CW01648276

Cricket Dreaming

Cricket Dreaming

The Rites of Summer

Barry Nicholls

Published by Brolga Publishing Pty Ltd
ABN 46 063 962 443
PO Box 12544
A'Beckett St
Melbourne, VIC, 8006
Australia
email: markzocchi@brolgapublishing.com.au

All rights reserved. No part of this publication may be reproduced, stored in a retrieval system or transmitted in any form or by any means electronic, mechanical, photocopying, recording or otherwise without prior permission from the publisher.

Copyright © Barry Nicholls

National Library of Australia
Cataloguing-in-Publication entry

Nicholls, Barry.
Cricket dreaming : the rites of summer / Barry Nicholls.
9781921221897 (pbk.)

Nicholls, Barry.
Cricket fans--Australia--Biography.
Autobiographical memory.

796.3580994

Printed in Indonesia
Cover Design by David Khan
Typeset and designed by Diana Evans

For Ann, Jacy, Ambrose and Harry

Contents

Opening the Batting •

Middle order •

All round status •

Stumps •

In the Clubhouse •

Acknowledgments

Whenever a project like this comes together there are many people to thank.

Firstly to Ann and our children Jacy, Ambrose and Harry, thanks for your support, patience and distractions! To Bernard Whimpress, editor of *Baggy Green Journal of Australian Cricket*, who advised on and published some of these stories. *Cricket Lore*'s Richard Hill did the same and I appreciate both Bernard and Richard's encouragement. To Chris Hamilton for his support and view that 'the glass is half full rather than half empty' regarding my writing and life in general. To Ashford Cricket Club's stalwart Chris Evans for helping iron out the memories of England. Dad offered some great suggestions while Nick Moschetta also provided some useful information. Warwick Franks provided encouragement and cast an eye over the text. The Whitty family was generous and hospitable in allowing me to visit their house, as did the late Les Hill. Thanks to John Harms for his sense of humour and foreword.

Brolga's Diana Evans has done a wonderful job editing the book and I thank her and the team at Brolga for their support for this project. To Peter Cornwall thanks again for your help.

Part of the chapter 'Cricket in Australia Beyond the Traditional Boundary' first appeared in *Wisden Cricketer's Almanack Australia.*

Finally I must give a note of appreciation to the cricketers, coaches and officials from all strata of cricket society. Without you there would be no stories.

Acknowledgments

*F*oreword

Had I not already known, I'd have worked out from his fine book, *Cricket Dreaming*, that Barry Nicholls and I were pretty close to the same age. And of a very similar sensibility. Particularly where cricket is concerned.

Which is interesting because we grew up 2000 kilometres apart. Yet his cricket experience, his cricket dreaming, is so similar to mine. He was a schoolboy in suburban Adelaide; I enjoyed a happy sporting childhood on Queensland's Darling Downs. His father threw balls at him, teaching him the elements of batsmanship; so did mine (particularly defence, sadly). Barry yearned for proper cricket matches. So did I, where there were two batsmen, both wearing pads. Test cricketers were his summer heroes. They were also mine.

This is the nature of a strong culture, and Australian cricket culture in the 1970s was just that: strong. There were things in cricket which appealed broadly, and created a common experience, a common understanding, before we ever thought about it. Barry Nicholls's experience is the experience of so many. We all dreamed of playing for Australia.

But the parallels are not mere coincidences and similarities. They are more profound than that. Both of us were caught by the mystery of cricket. We were captivated by the thrill of making runs and taking wickets, by the desire to make our way in the game. And, as we got older, by the need to understand what that mystery was, and why cricket had such a grip on us, why it provided such meaning. Surely it was more than mere ego of personal striving? I hope it was.

I kept shaking my head at the closeness of our experience. I was first taken to a Test match in January 1971, against England, at the MCG while on holidays in Melbourne. Bill Lawry declared when Rod Marsh was on 92. Barry's first was the very next Test in Adelaide: the debut of one D.K. Lillee.

Around that time Barry tried to bowl leg-spinners. So did I, copying Kerry O'Keefe, only my young wrist was so supple I couldn't bowl anything but wrong 'uns.

The 1974-75 Ashes series was formative. I listened on my pocket radio to Doug Walters's century in a session at the WACA while I mowed Mrs. McGrath's lawn, for which I received the sum of $2. I made it inside to see the last few overs on our old black and white TV. I have the clearest memory of the first morning of the first Test at the 'Gabba. We boys from Oakey State Primary stood at the school gate in white Grand Slam shirts, white stubbies, white floppies, and white Volleys, waiting for one of the parents to pick us up to drive us into Toowoomba to take on Wilsonton, or Rangeville. I had my radio and we are listening as Ian and Greg Chappell were batting and Tony Greig was niggling them.

Just as it has for Barry, the first World Cup final provided one of the vivid memories of my childhood. The night was so long. It was midnight, frosty outside, and the West Indies were still batting. And I was still up. I think I lasted the full distance until the Australians fell short in the run chase, though I felt guilty and decadent, staying up all night.

This book will remind older readers of so much. Of Size 4 and harrow size cricket bats (a term I had forgotten); of sausage gloves (they were so much more sophisticated than the green-spiked gloves of school kits); of the board game Test Match.

This is not a self-indulgent memoir. It is carried by a tone of inquiry, delving into the past and commenting on events and issues through to the present. It also carries the lament that those times have passed, and we are now blessed with hamstrings and eyesight which prevent us from doing what we once could do, or sort of do. And although we enjoyed a few moments of cricket glory (he at a higher level than me: he twice batted on the Adelaide Oval proper, I only ever batted on No. 2) we both have played cricket at a high enough level to know how brilliant Doug Walters and Dennis Lillee were.

But most of all it captures the game we love, offering critical insight and enthusiastic celebration. I can imagine Barry throwing balls at his own young bloke(s).

Just like me.

— John Harms

You haven't lived until you've opened the batting for Australia

– found on a toilet door in country South Australia

Introduction

This is really a book of memories from a time when Twenty20 was considered perfect vision and cricket's base – the much lampooned International Cricket Council (ICC) – was firmly ensconced in London. Australian cricketers were larrikins who wore long hair and without meaning to, provided journalists across the world with worthwhile soundbites. It was when cigarette marketing (rather than fast food) dominated the advertising and when you could watch cricket from a hill instead of being quarantined into stands or corporate tents.

Security meant a few friendly blokes who kept an eye on the pitch after the match and streakers added levity to the occasion. Big screens were something you went to the cinema to see and disco's association with cricket ended with a visiting team filling in for a Sydney disc jockey at a night club. For some the era of the 1970s and '80s endure as the time when cricket was played by real men who showed their chest hair and would think twice before wearing a helmet. For others it's an archaic reminder of what led us to where we are now.

This is the story of a cricket fan's journey from one who had connections from the inner sanctum with those who played the game. It is an outsider's look at the inside.

Now whenever India star Sachin Tendulkar goes out to bat, close to a billion people are said to watch his every footstep. Cricket is not as dominant in Australian culture but is the main sporting focus each summer. For many the cricket commentary helps make up the soundtrack of the summer. The unconverted wonder what all the fuss is about, mystified about what drives men and women to spend days playing or watching a game that occupies so much time. Even to the converted the attraction can seem difficult to fathom. It is possible to play an entire match without touching the ball. Yet there are also moments of sublime grace, for both players and spectators, in the striking of a sweetly timed drive, the bowling of a perfect delivery, and the taking of an unlikely catch (or, in my case, any slip catch). When asked of the significance of his achievements, the dour former English opener Geoff Boycott once said the memory of scoring a hundred at Lord's would surely outlive that of bedding a Miss Universe. Oddly enough it's a sentiment many Australian men would agree with.

Cricket has a rich history that has become part of our folklore. It provides us with a window into our country's past. Like many sports it helps form friendships, 'opens doors' and creates an opportunity to travel. Each year hundreds of Australians go overseas to play cricket in various parts of the world. England is a common destination on a journey that's as much about life as it is about cricket. It's a rite of passage for many. Those few who 'make it' and break into the elite ranks of the sport become entrenched in another generation's memories. For the rest, we have the memories of the beer and the socialising.

LP Hartley began his famous 1953 novel, *The Go-Between* (which has a cricket match as its dramatic climax), with the words: 'The past is a foreign country: they do things differently there.'

This seems doubly true in the case of cricket. For those growing up in the 1930s and '40s, it was all about Bradman, or the debonair style of Keith Miller. The Baby Boomers admired the flamboyance and aggressive captaincy of Richie Benaud. The Generation Xers saw Benaud in a different light, more often than not in a beige coat on Channel Nine, fronting the increasingly commercialised coverage of the game. But those events, like many pockets of history, are fast becoming distant, buried in the vast number of limited over matches.

One of cricket's greatest legacies is its memories. Remembering our heroes from childhood reminds us what it is to be young, full of promise and aiming for the stars. Our heroes grow old, but in our eyes they remain forever young. To quote Gordie Lachance in the movie *Stand by Me*, 'There are no heroes like the ones we have when we are twelve years old.'

For me that time included the Chappell era from 1971 to '83. It was a period when cricket recaptured the Australian sporting market with the advent of Kerry Packer's World Series Cricket. The revolution won over a legion of fans – young and old, male and female. Cricket became fashionable again. The game steeped in tradition finally moved into the modern era and world administrators would follow.

From 1977 Australians soaked up two seasons of international cricket in one as official and Packer matches operated alongside each other. The way we watched the game also changed. Cricket and American baseball became closer cousins not only in format but also in marketing. Players gained celebrity status. Coloured clothing and night cricket were introduced. Songs like 'C'mon Aussie C'mon' were part of the sell. Who could forget the line, 'Hookesy's clearing pickets and the Chappells' eyes have got that killer gleam'? Suddenly watching cricket on television changed. We could watch the match from a variety of camera angles. We could even hear the players sledging and the sound of the wickets rattling because of a microphone strategically placed behind the stumps. Cricket had become a conduit for the latest in sporting technology.

Player politics were suddenly more obvious to the average fan. Divisions formed between the establishment and those who 'sold their cricketing soul' to WSC. Players who wouldn't have made it into the top two Australian teams were suddenly wearing the baggy green.

Many of us remember what we were doing when Doug Walters hit the lanky and robotic Bob Willis for six off the last ball of the day to bring up his ton in an Ashes Test. We cheered even louder when Kim Hughes struck a famous hundred and then Dennis Lillee bowled Viv Richards off the last ball of the day in the Boxing Day Test of 1981.

Like all history, cricket provides stories of triumph and tragedy. Death looms large in the game's language. Batsmen are victims, bowlers target individuals and pitches can be described as minefields. Finality is the essence of the game where second chances are limited if they exist at all.

Cricket's association with death began well before the tragic passing of Pakistan coach Bob Woolmer at the 2007 World Cup. David Frith's *Silence of the Heart* revealed a surprisingly high suicide rate among cricketers, much more prevalent than in the general population. Cricket's history features its share of unusual deaths from the murder of New South Wales's Dr Claude Tozer in 1920 to Martin Bedkober's fatal injury in a Brisbane grade match in the 1970s.

Cricket in Australia is at last reaching beyond its traditional boundaries, and playing a greater part in the lives of Aboriginal people. Former Queensland fast bowler Eddie Gilbert, an Aboriginal man from Cherbourg mission in Queensland, was a victim of racism in the 1930s. More than twenty years after his death, Queensland has become a key state for indigenous cricket with success at the national carnival staged annually in Alice Springs. Statues saluting Gilbert's achievements now stand in Cherbourg and Brisbane. Former Australian off-spinner Ashley Mallett has even called for Australia Day to take place on February 13, the national day of apology for past wrongdoings to Aboriginal people.

Cricket is poised at a critical juncture with the lucrative wave of Twenty20 matches upon us. The way ahead, with the growing dominance of limited overs cricket and a power base set in the subcontinent, is unknown. We do know, however, what has gone and the forces that shaped it.

Chapter 1

The Beginning

I am standing in the middle of my school oval. The atmosphere is pulsating, very much alive, like that of a crowded swimming pool in summer. There is a buzz of excitement all around me. Children are making noise as they play all sorts of games; some are on the ground with marbles, others running around playing chasey. A number climb on playground equipment. Others simply run randomly.

It is a beautiful sunny day in October 1969. Each moment of lunchtime is to be savoured. That year man has walked on the moon, and my favourite plastic lunar model still sits on the shelf above my bed. But now just a few months later, Neil Armstrong's 'One small step' seems insignificant compared to my newfound love of cricket.

I stand as part of the cricketing community, spread across the school oval. Being seven years old, my enthusiasm is overwhelming. I am so eager I jump up and down as I wait for my chance to bat. Like my classmates I am only allowed to play at the bottom of the oval. Looking toward the upper primary I see the future. The big kids are using the trees that line the metal fence next to school as wickets. They are playing different games from us. The action is much quicker and there is more shouting. We have a teacher who organises us and says when it's our turn to bat. The activity is contained and it doesn't matter if you get out or not in order to keep batting. They play real cricket on the top half of the oval.

I can't wait to play using the trees as wickets, and jumpers at the non-striker's end. I'm not sure when or how this tradition began, but it allows for the best possible use of the space. The dirt in front of the 'wicket' is worn, making the ground resemble a turf pitch. The games line up parallel to one another with a gap of about two metres between trees. Conflicts occur between different grades as balls are hit across the path of incoming bowlers and fielders. There is no video replay or third umpire to adjudicate the close run outs. There are no umpires at all. The biggest kids dictate, or the boy who owns the bat and ball. Any argument soon dissipates as the action moves on. It looks great.

The siren sounds, signalling the upper primary to go inside. The oval empties, but at a much slower rate than it filled. At the southern end of Linden Park Demonstration School, the oval still hums with the life and vibrancy of children at play.

It is in this transition period that I have my epiphany. I love footy but cricket is my game. Reflection is rare when you are seven years old, but cricket has that effect. I soon discover the game has manifested itself in my life in a variety of ways. I start commentating while standing in front of a mirror practising my batting. Keeping my elbow up for defensive strokes and rolling my wrists for cuts and pulls have become priorities. Pocket money is spent on cricket magazines and Christmas and birthday wish lists are dominated by requests for equipment, books and games.

When cricket is on the television I sit huddled in the corner recording the play in my small green score book. Scoring is a secret code with its dots and crosses passed on by Dad.

Common ground is found at school with like-minded classmates. My use of cricketing language expands exponentially. I even understand averages when the maths teacher goes through the answers. I long for some cricket words in my weekly spelling list, but few eventuate.

By the time I am ten my love for cricket has turned to a full-blown obsession. I see cricket in everything. Endless hours in front of the mirror give me a rock solid defence. Word spreads about my ability to stonewall. I find it hard to score any runs while I occupy the crease. One day at lunchtime a teacher on yard duty pretends to dust cobwebs off me while I am batting.

The obsession develops. I often refer to a tall old man with a long grey beard called WG and talk of cricket's golden age. I am the only one of my peers still outraged by the use of Bodyline tactics in 1932-33. I use Bill Woodfull's phrase 'there's two teams out there and only one's playing cricket' when I think the opposition isn't playing by the rules. I still manage to have friends.

And then Greg Chappell visits the school for a coaching clinic.

I know all about him. I can recite his scores from the '72 Ashes tour (24, 23, 131, 7 not out, 26, 72, 12, 13, 113 and 16). I can imitate his unorthodox way of hitting the ball from middle and leg through mid-wicket, or at least I can in front of the mirror. When he scored 197 against the Rest of the World and leaned his head against his bat to rest toward the end of the day's play, I was watching on television.

They say knowledge is power but it gets me nowhere. The coaching clinic is for grade sevens only. On the big day, I sneak out of class for a 'toilet break' to catch a glimpse. I make it as far as the oval's edge before a stern look from the year seven coach has me backtracking. Chappell is standing hatless talking to a group of kids sitting on the ground. The parents gather to one side. He is holding a bat, demonstrating straight bat shots with one hand and then grabs the blade with both hands and answers questions while twirling his bat. It is a bittersweet moment. I make my way back to class, occasionally turning around as I reluctantly retreat. When the school day ends I run to the oval only to see parents dispersing and Chappell's van pulling away.

I formulate my aim, which seems very straight forward at the time, to open the batting for Australia. The future has been marked and cricket is right in the middle of it.

Chapter 2

The Appeal of Cricket: a Tale of Two Tests

Learning how to appreciate Test cricket is an art. It's a gradual process that has to be savoured and reflected upon. My introduction came in the form of a boring Test match during an equally dull series in which all but two of the seven games were drawn (one Test was washed out without a ball being bowled). RS Whitington in his book about the series, *Captains Outrageous*, described the contest as containing 'perhaps the least attractive Test matches Australians have attended'. It's worth considering that Whitington also covered the 1958-59 England tour. This was when cricket was played at a glacial speed.

In 1970-71 RS Whitington described the opposing captains, Billy Lawry and Ray Illingworth, as having 'dismissed all delight, all adventure… they drained the colour from its old time tapestry.' Such was the climate of Ashes cricket in late January 1971 when my family was among more than twenty thousand spectators at the sixth Test of the series. The match reports describe the weather as cool and windy. It was the first time I saw Adelaide Oval. The ground's surface seemed to stretch forever and looked as smooth as the bowling greens we drove past on the way home from school where elderly people in white uniforms spent their leisurely afternoons.

We arrived at the ground just after the England captain Ray Illingworth won the toss. Soon the visitors' names appeared on the old Adelaide Oval scoreboard at a frantic pace. When play started there was a strange hush between deliveries and a sense of anticipation as to how the match might unfold. It was the biggest crowd I had ever seen, providing a montage of colours and shapes around the ground.

Our family sat in a grandstand on small uncomfortable wooden seats jammed in close together. Mum had packed sandwiches. There was also the treat of a soft drink and an ice-cream from the canteen behind the grandstand.

It seemed an important occasion. When I looked across to the packed Adelaide Oval Members', plumes of cigarette smoke rose above men dressed in suits. The spectators were divided into different areas of formalities. During the afternoon we went for a walk past the two grassed 'hills' near the scoreboard at the northern end of the ground. The crowd barracked differently there. They were loud and became noisier as the afternoon wore on. Shirtless men threw plastic beer cups into the air to entertain themselves. The police moved in quickly. Whenever a young woman walked past, a great roar erupted. The fewer clothes she was wearing the louder the cheer.

But these were just peripheries; we were there of course for the cricket.

The day's play was very slow but it demonstrated the attrition of cricket, a game I was learning had its own subtleties. By stumps only two wickets had fallen, one just as our family walked from the ground. We heard the cheers signalling the late fall of John Edrich, whose 130 guided England to 276 at the close. I asked Dad what the noise meant. 'Probably what we've been waiting all day to see,' was his reply. He didn't look impressed.

Our premature departure was to satisfy my three older brothers who struggled to develop a connection with cricket. My brothers' disaffection grew steadily throughout the day as Geoffrey Boycott cobbled together 58 in more than three hours. He was eventually run out in pursuit of a quick single.

I later discovered it was a rare to see Boycott dismissed this way. He was judged by many an opponent and even some team mates to be a selfish prat, and a mistaken call would normally see his batting partner heading back to the pavilion. This time he misjudged Ian Chappell's arm when he threw the wicket down from mid-on. Boycott also misjudged the crowd's sense of justice, lingering at the crease after being given out by the South Australian umpire, Max O'Connell. Eventually England's opener left the ground after prompting from the rookie of the Australian side and home ground

'On ya bike.' Greg Chappell gives Boycott a send off, Adelaide Oval, 1970-71.

favourite, Greg Chappell. The photos of the incident in the newspapers the next day were dramatic; although I'm sure it caused a laugh among the players. Boycott made up for his petulance in the second innings, scoring an unbeaten 119 as the match ended in another draw. That summer Boycott had the last laugh, scoring 657 Test runs at an average of 93.

I could say that the drama created by Boycott's dismissal on that first day helped spark my interest in cricket, but that would be lying. I don't remember any of it. I was down at the drink stall with Mum escaping the stuffiness of our seats in the stand when it happened.

On reflection the first day of the Adelaide Test was when cricket began a long line of examinations for me. The game was daring me to continue my interest. The experience confirmed my brothers' views that cricket was a boring waste of time. But for me there was something appealing about the struggle of the contest and the game's formalities. Rituals gave the occasion a sense of grandeur. Drinks breaks signalled a sudden movement of people. Sessions closed with the bails being gently tipped off the stumps by men in white coats. There was a silence over the ground when play resumed. The simple sounds of the day stood out. Gentle clapping from the Members welcomed players to the field. Wickets, particularly English ones, were greeted with a crescendo of noise echoing around the ground. As the day progressed captains moved their players around the field in a subtle manner while the batsmen sought solidarity in each other's company in the middle of the pitch.

Undeterred by the lack of action, I asked to be taken to the Rest of the World clash against Australia the next season.

The cricket outing this time with Mum was well planned to ensure we had seats in the John Creswell stand (where the Bradman stand now overlooks the oval). I listened to the first three days of the game on radio, hoping it wouldn't end before the day we had tickets – day four.

Despite my monitoring, the match was all but over when the big day arrived. This time the grandstand was close to empty. Only six thousand turned up to watch the final rites as Hylton Ackerman and Rohan Kanhai finished off a meagre chase of 146. The Rest of the World scored the winning runs just after lunch. Garry Sobers, the man I had come especially to watch, stayed in his street clothes. When I looked over to the Rest of the World's dressing room I could see Sobers happily chatting to his team mates as if planning a round of golf for later that afternoon. The highlight of the day consisted of eating a pie and a pasty from the cafeteria beneath the stand in the area that doubled as an indoor cricket centre. It was little consolation for not seeing Sobers bat.

I never got the chance to watch Sobers bat live during his prime, but I did witness him bat briefly in an exhibition match at Parkinson Oval at the home of my club, Kensington. It was more than a decade after he had played his final Test. Sobers scored only three runs before skying a ball to cover, giving one club bowler something to talk about for the rest of his life. The crowd lining the boundary let out a disappointed sigh when a laughing Sobers was dismissed. It gave me an indication of the expectation he faced whenever he walked onto a cricket field. At least I saw him bat once.

Adelaide's experience of 'Test cricket' that summer was greatly anticipated. Earlier that season Dennis Lillee announced his arrival on the international scene, while a match later Sobers opened a new generation's eyes to his brilliance. When Lillee took eight for 29 off seven overs in the first Test in Perth he sounded a warning to batsmen around the world. This was Lillee before an injured back almost ended his career. When he ran in to bowl he looked like a god. His long dark hair jumped around out of sync with his arms that splayed outwards with each energetic stride. The bounce and pace Lillee extracted from the hard and fast WACA wicket blew the tourists away. The Rest of the World followed on after a dismal 59. They didn't do much better in the second innings as Australia marched away with the match by an innings and 11 runs.

Sobers made 0 and 33 in Perth and then followed up with a golden duck in the first innings of the second match in Melbourne. When Sobers walked off he surprisingly wore a huge smile as if to say, 'Have I got a surprise for you?' It seemed a strange way to react.

The response was an unforgettable second innings of 254 which lit up the MCG despite the efforts of Dennis Lillee. In doing so Sobers patented the perfect knock. He batted with such fluency it was like watching an animation. If ever there was an example of a player in what sports psychologists call 'a state of flow' this was it. Coaches still use footage of the innings as an attacking template.

Sobers's innings also helped add charm to former leg-spinner Kerry O'Keeffe's claims as the spinner who didn't. O'Keeffe's 27 wicket-less overs during Sobers's onslaught cost 121. If you watch the old black and white footage you'll often see O'Keeffe standing at the bowlers end with one arm folded across his body while the other hand scratches his chin. The expression on his face is one of bewilderment. It was similar to the look on Richie Benaud's face eleven years earlier when Sobers hit his bowling all around the Gabba for a hundred on the first day of the first Tied Test. Benaud at least had the grace to smile and clap the batsmen from time to time.

Sobers's masterpiece was analysed by cricket writers whose superlatives were accompanied by the scorer's wagon wheel chart which revealed the diversity of his stroke play. Nowadays the knock would be celebrated by the release of a Sobers print. It would be sold as a 'limited edition' of 2,540 copies, with 254 special gold-plated copies signed by the great all-rounder. Sobers's performance was given an endorsement from Sir Donald Bradman, describing it as the best innings he had seen on Australian soil. Sobers smiled that day and appeared to do so for the rest of the season. So did Bradman. It was Bradman, as Chairman of the Australian Cricket Board, who had asked Sobers to forgo his final season with South Australia in the Sheffield Shield to captain the Rest of the World.

In his role, Bradman had also received advice from Australian Prime Minister Billy McMahon regarding the South African tour of Australia, as revealed by Gideon Haigh and David Frith's *Inside Story Unlocking Australian Cricket's Archives.* After this he made a reluctant and pragmatic endorsement of the decision to cancel, as security made it impossible. As an eight year old, the political turbulence was lost on me, although I wondered why pictures of Australian protestors at the rugby clash with South Africa were on the television. One of our local grounds, Norwood Oval, was the scene of demonstrations during an international under lights.

The Rest of the World side was unlike any other to tour Australia. It had a cultural mix that included players from England, South Africa, Pakistan, India, West Indies and New Zealand. In the summer of 1971-72 I was introduced to players such as Farokh Engineer, Hylton Ackerman, Intikhab Alam, Zaheer Abbas, Bishan Bedi and Rohan Kanhai, and had a first look at the six-foot-seven South African all-rounder Tony Greig. They had exotic names and were wonderful cricketers who were largely unknown to me and my friends, whose cricket diet had centred on the Ashes. I didn't even consider the politics of a war between India and Pakistan and the effect it could have had on team unity.

The series was a contest involving some of the best players in the world but, like World Series Cricket, it was never granted Test status. It seems an injustice even if for no other reason than to allow Sobers's 254 its rightful place in cricket's history.

Test cricket's early live experiences had offered little on-field excitement. It didn't matter. I had begun to discover cricket's soul and the many storylines that lay beneath the surface for those playing and watching the game.

Chapter 3

The Ball

A cricket ball in an old stocking sits heavy on the ground. It's trying to swing in the breeze. The heat is blistering on a typical January day at home in Alice Springs. A hot northerly wind is blowing and the temperature hovers menacingly near 40 degrees Celsius. It's still early in the morning when I open the screen door, but the heat hits me like a wall. Better to get used to it straight away. Although it's shaded, the concrete outside the back door is hot enough underfoot to make you want to move quickly. The heat is so enveloping it feels like putting your head in an oven. Activity is restricted to either just after sunrise or late into the night.

At the moment of the heat's greeting, I am returned to days when sweat and the smell of sunscreen were a constant reminder of weekend life. Only in my mid-twenties did I begin to question spending entire summer weekends playing cricket. In spite of the testing conditions in the intense summer heat, the sense of camaraderie and feeling of being physically drained after the match made the whole experience worthwhile.

I glance across our back patio to where a cricket ball swings from a rafter. Suddenly it feels as if I'm in a time warp to the 1970s, living at my parents' houses. It was the first few years after their divorce. In a family of four boys my 'only child' status happened overnight. My mother and two eldest brothers had moved out separately while my other brother spent most of his spare time at his girlfriend's place. The ball in the stocking was a new companion as I commentated on imaginary Test matches or sang along with songs on a small transistor.

The bomb of my parents divorce in the mid-1970s was part of the first wave of unhappy couples who made the most of the Whitlam Government's new 'no faults' divorce legislation. Until then you had had to prove infidelity. The change, I imagine, upset private detectives earning their keep from surveillance of philandering partners. Nowadays, when I see the frail, old and dignified man who is Gough Whitlam on television, I don't think of the withdrawal of Australian troops from Vietnam, a potential double dissolution or even the ultimate riposte of 'nothing will save the Governor-General', but instead my family life turned upside down. The 'It's Time,' political theme that helped propel the 'new saviour' into office was true for me but not for political reasons.

Admittedly, after my parents' divorce life became more peaceful, or so it seemed. It was the practicalities that really stung. I was jettisoned from our family house to the adjacent suburb of Glen Osmond for the weekend. During the week I lived in a two-bedroom unit in Beulah Park near my new school, away from my old neighbourhood friends. The new school was a private college where I was acutely aware of not being part of the 'in crowd'. It was an uncertain time for a 13 year old going through the usual pubescent blues. I was now one of the few kids in the school with two homes, where the second one wasn't a plush beach house by the coast.

The trauma worsened when my parents saw each other for the weekly 'drop off'. Habitually, I accidentally left vital items such as school shoes, ties and socks behind during the weekly transfer, until it was agreed to duplicate certain items, namely the less expensive ones such as socks and ties.

I love my Mum and Dad, it was just they didn't share that love for each other. Needless to say when they were forced to meet, a squabble ensued and I was sharply reminded of why my home life had changed. After their weekly meetings, I wondered at how many different things people could argue about, only later realising the topic wasn't the problem.

All of these reminders from a simple cricket ball in a stocking.

The first time I set up the ball was at Mum's place. There wasn't much of a yard and what grass did exist was within the concrete tiles that extended out from a small garage. Each night I visited the corner store deli where I bought the now defunct *Adelaide News*, a litre of cola and a custard tart as part of a post-school ritual. The man who owned the shop was always happy to see me, which wasn't surprising given the amount I was spending. He was an English bloke with jet black slick-backed hair who talked about his love of the speedway. I could relate to this because I used to read the English comic *Tiger and Scorcher* which featured stories and pictures about speedways at huge stadiums like Wembley. We would talk about sport and he said one day he'd like to take me to the speedway but it never eventuated.

Dad stayed at our old house for a few months until it was sold. Once the finances were settled he moved a block or so up the road. At times I walked from Dad's new place to our old home just to remember what life was like when we were a family. I often wondered if anyone was using the concrete cricket pitch we had in our back yard. One day I hung a cricket ball in one of Mum's stockings out on Dad's veranda. I don't know what my old man thought of his ex-wife's stocking swaying in the breeze outside the lounge window, but I suspect it was a reminder he could have done without.

The play area at Dad's was small but not as limiting as Mum's. The backyard had an open garage and lawn with glass greenhouses adjoining one of the neighbour's fences. We could still play cricket, but I missed the gully from our old house. What was left of the windows in the unused greenhouse didn't last long. At least it confirmed that my straight driving skills were improving.

When I hit the ball on the stocking on Dad's veranda, I could choose the perspective of hitting toward the neighbour's house or in the direction of the lounge room window. This had the advantage of allowing me to check my stroke in the window's reflection. If I hit the other way I was often stopped when our neighbour Max, a retired farmer from the south-east of South Australia, said hello. He'd always ask how my cricket or the family dog, Snoopy, were going. Our brown cocker spaniel used to spend his afternoons sleeping in the sun in Max's garden. Max, by then close to 70, was a gentle and friendly man who toiled away in his garden each day under a big straw hat.

Now the humble ball in a stocking has at last hit the commercial world. One of my entrepreneurial friends has marketed a basic ball-in-a-stocking concept and is selling it world wide, sugar-coated with images of Bradman and the water tank. When I heard this, I wondered why I hadn't thought of it.

Chapter 4

Boyhood Dreams

Cricket in the early 1970s prompts images of the moustached, long-haired Dennis Lillee bounding in with his arms flailing wildly, pounding one down to a stoic Geoffrey Boycott. But for me it was much simpler, playing on the many instant pitches that snaked their way around my school oval in the frantic lunchtime rush.

A bird's eye view would have resembled a cartoon where an artist has tried to fit as many pictures of cricketers into one image as possible, like in a *Where's Wally?* book. It looked disorganised but games took on their own logic. Tippy-go added to the frenzy of dropped catches and disputed run-outs that dotted the landscape of these lunchtime contests.

No one ever used the concrete cricket pitch.

When it was wet the older kids moved the game to the elevated asphalt tennis courts (where every sport but tennis was played). The oversized and unused gate was the wicket and any snick behind was out. It was like batting against the 1974-75 Australian team; a chorus of intimidation and an inevitable cluster of fieldsmen greeted anyone refusing to walk. Decisions were quickly resolved and the game moved on.

By grade six it was a relief to play proper cricket. Until

then average cricket – a game where you couldn't get out and everyone batted and bowled for the same number of overs – provided the only organised option. It was an apt name for a game that stunted the growth of good players. When you are a school sports nut you want real things, like getting out in cricket and finals in footy, but I was denied both. (In grade five, I played in the Linden Park under 10A's. We went through the entire season undefeated, but the organisers thought finals were 'too competitive'. The year didn't end with the crowning glory of a grand final win and lap of the ground carrying the premiership flag and cup but instead an easy victory against the weakest side in the competition. It was a hollow end to the season.)

Young Barry at bat.

We all dreamed of one day wearing the baggy green. In quieter moments at home I practised the way Ian Chappell left the wicket, taking his gloves off with an elongated sweep of his arms. The Australian captain looked like he was angrily swatting a fly. It looked aggressive, but it showed me the real pain of getting out.

After two years of 'full rules' primary cricket (except for having to retire at 30) and as I neared the end of primary school, I felt that the journey to full cricketer had begun. I had the demented Chappelli squint at the sun, heavy masticating and upturned collar as I walked to the wicket. In preparation for my first innings of 'real cricket', I practised the walk up and down the stairs of our two-story house when I was playing the board game Test Match.

The popular 1970s game contained two dials you clicked over. It showed whether the ball you bowled had been hit for runs or got a wicket and was set on a cardboard backdrop that looked like a hybrid of Adelaide Oval and a circus tent. The cover featured a batsman with a high back lift pouncing out to hit the ball. It looked more like baseball than cricket. You needed no cricketing nous or skill to play. Perhaps that explains its popularity. I loved the crisp smell of the game's box and the clean swishing noise of the dials when I clicked them over in anticipation. It was a game of options that randomly fell your way. By the same method the bowlers 'delivered' long hops, bouncers, half-volleys and no balls. As a batsman the dangers of being bowled, LBW, caught or run out lurked at every swish (no stumpings or hit wicket). (I purchased the game again when I was in my thirties. 'Oh he'll like that one,' the store owner said, assuming I had bought it for a child, which in a sense I had.) Indoor games were great when it rained but we longed for the real thing when the sun shone.

The chance to play proper cricket arrived unexpectedly in grade five. The debut for my house team came about because a school camp had depleted player numbers. I can't remember who I played on the small Linden Park number two oval nestled among a row of green leafy suburban homes, but I remember thinking it was the most important day of my cricket life.

I dreamed of a spectacular debut. After the initial threat of rain, leaden skies lifted and we were on. The top and middle order failed and the moment of truth arrived. With the shiny red 'compo' ball dominating I took guard, attempting to scrape a mark on the concrete pitch with my Dunlop Volley shoes. Looking up, I realised the fieldsmen, of which there seemed to be many, were decidedly bigger than my classmates. Anxiety set in. I shouldn't have worried. It was all over in a hurry. The bowler had a long run, the shuffle of his shoes echoing in my ears. He moved across the T-shaped start of the concrete pitch. There was a red blur, more bounce than I had expected, a bottom edge and the sound of metal clanging. Out first ball. It was the first time I heard the death rattle; in this case, the clang of metal stumps.

The second day's play the next week was washed out, but it didn't matter; I was a real cricketer now.

After Christmas 1974, I was the proud owner of my first bat. Until then, I'd used the family one Dad had bought a couple of years earlier. I touched my new Slazenger bat for the first time as my family unwrapped presents. Later in the day we listened to news that a cyclone called Tracy had wiped out the northern city of Darwin. This distant national disaster failed to resonate with my eleven-year-old mind. Instead I concentrated on playing with my new bat. My bat had a varnished cover but I oiled it anyway, from the bottom up, and bounced an older leather ball on its surface to ease it in. My new bat looked like the one that Alan Knott was using in a famous photo. The shot showed the English stumper caught behind off Dennis Lillee during the 1972 Ashes tour. In it

Lillee was half-turned, looking exhausted yet relieved as he completed his leap. Knott was bent forward, resigned to dismissal. Marsh was hurling the ball skywards as the slip cordon all jumped as one. You could see the striped symbol on Knott's guilt-ridden blade.

I was one of the lucky ones. My bat had been properly picked out. It was the right size – harrow – and light enough for me to play shots square of the wicket. Like most kids my age I scored runs with cross bat strokes like the cut and pull shots where I could use the pace of the ball. I tried to play the cut shot the way I'd seen ill-fated Archie Jackson in a black and white photo. Jackson's arms were half extended as he executed a perfectly balanced stroke. It looked dignified like a cover drive, only more refined. I mastered the cut, because of the weight of my first bat. (That and the fact that Dad had a habit of bowling short outside off stump.) Parents often buy their kids a bat that they are supposed to grow into. The only problem is that the bat is often so heavy it can't be used properly. The kid normally takes up bowling or gives up altogether.

Obsessively driven to master technique, I prided myself on an ability to play straight. Once the coach of an opposition team told me my backlift wasn't straight. I took it as a personal insult. He said it explained why I struggled to gain power driving. He recommended a practise where I had to stand hard up next to a fence and lift the bat back with one hand. It was supposed to train you to bring the bat back straight and not toward the slips. It seemed to work but created an odd sight when I tried it.

In those days, leg spin bowling was about as fashionable as a short back and sides haircut. It didn't matter; I experimented with it anyway. Dad showed me the basic grip and talked about his glory days at Cowandilla Primary School in the western suburbs of Adelaide. He showed me the book presented to him at the school assembly by Clarrie Grimmett. It was for taking the most wickets in a season. I suppose none of the teachers thought of getting Clarrie to sign Dad's prize. He told me how he saw Grimmett ride through the school gates that day on a bicycle with his trousers rolled up.

Then one day it happened, I accidentally bowled a wrong'un in the backyard nets. Dad's face lit up when he saw it. He said that not many people could bowl a googly. I felt I was one of the chosen ones born with this special gift. The world was my oyster. This was until I discovered that having mastered the googly I was unable to bowl a leg break. I persisted and took some wickets with looping deliveries that bounced to unexpected heights on concrete wickets. It all went awry the day I was crashed around the Hay Road Oval for 24 in one eight ball over. That morning I discovered the loneliness of a leg-spinner, standing in the middle of an oval with fielders scattered around the boundary. It didn't matter where I bowled, the oversized kid at the other end continued to hit the ball either over or to the boundary. The increasing noise of the cheers and laughter from the batting side added to the humiliation.

I decided it was time to return to the mirror to work on my cover drive.

I enjoyed my time at school but classwork was never a priority. I tried reading *The Lion, the Witch and the Wardrobe* but the first book that captured my imagination was Ian Chappell's *Tigers among the Lions*. The introduction explains the unusual title. It told of how Chappell and a number of his team mates on the 1972 England tour played for teams that had tigers in their club emblem. Australia's key strike bowler Dennis Lillee was nicknamed 'Tiger', while his fellow WA players also had yellow and black in their state colours. Ian Chappell's state team mates Ashley Mallett and Greg Chappell, who played for Glenelg, also called the Tigers, and a pattern emerges. To top it off, the manager of the 1972 tour was also a former Richmond (Tigers) footballer, Ray Steele. Chappell noted the Australian Tigers had caused an upset by winning two Tests and drawing the series and causing 'consternation in the English Lions' den'. This symbolism appealed to me and for the first time I read something in a book that engaged me.

It's too long ago for me to remember much more about it, but if I open the book now, memories of life as an eleven year old momentarily come flooding back; thoughts of leg-spinners, cover drives and an old Slazenger bat.

Chapter 5

A Pitch in Time

Made up of just twenty or so metres of turf, the cricket pitch has a lexicon of its own. Assessments of the pitch become crucial in conversations between players. Phrases used to describe a pitch – such as 'keeping low', 'flat as the Hume Highway', 'will turn later in the day', ' has life in it', and 'likely to turn nasty once it dries out' – may sound foreign to the uninitiated, but echo with familiarity around the country every Saturday afternoon.

When groundsmen talk about cricket pitches they speak in serious tones. It's a bit like listening to a museum curator discussing a gallery or exhibition. The quality of the pitch is a fundamental barometer as to how groundsmen are judged. Groundsmen have special remedies and ways of preparing a wicket. They like to put their face next to the pitch when examining the surface. It's as if they are communicating with the turf.

Regardless of a pitch's appearance you never know how it will perform until the first ball is bowled. Until then, nervous batsmen will ruminate about the pitch and how it might play. Any rain before match day will see them visiting the ground to inspect the wicket. (Batsmen dread a sticky wicket, but it's a bowler's best friend. They have been known to gather like vultures around it if there is the hint of moisture.) It was a habit so ingrained in me that even years after I'd stopped playing, I found it difficult to walk past an oval without wandering out to the middle to have a look at the pitch.

The pitch is like a magnet that draws cricketers to it. It is the first part of the ground players visit on match day; that is unless they have food on their mind. Then they will head straight to the dressing room to examine the offerings for afternoon tea. Experience taught me that if team mates were organising the refreshments this was a pointless visit. No matter how much you hoped, you knew that the same sad collection of barbecue snaps and iced vovos would make up the day's provisions.

The memories of a bad pitch stay with you for life and often create cricketing folklore. The stories normally arise from a batsman's bravery and skill in defying the conditions or a bowler's haul of wickets. I once played on a wicket that was so unpredictable that the first ball of the match skidded along the ground while the next one sprung violently from a good length, shattering my batting partner's helmet into many pieces. Luckily I wasn't facing. You could almost sense the incoming batsmen shuddering in the pavilion. For no obvious reason the pitch played perfectly well for the remainder of the match. Despite this, our batsmen struggled simply because they thought the pitch would be a nightmare.

Cricketers of all standards have a defining horror pitch. In the 1980s in Adelaide district cricket, one such story circulated about an Adelaide University C-grade team, made up mainly of Law and Arts students from the plush eastern suburbs. Playing away from their familiar scenic parkland city oval, in the working class suburb of Port Adelaide, they encountered a pitch prepared by Port Adelaide footballer Dave Granger. Standing at more than six feet, he was considered such a physical threat on the football field that he was known in football circles by the nickname 'Grave Danger'. After the first half hour of play, the University side, having been sent in to bat, was seven wickets down for 20. Just as the seventh wicket fell, and without any hint of irony, Granger wandered over and asked the players how they thought the pitch was playing. Fully aware of the groundsman's reputation, the young University team all smiled and nodded in agreement, vouching for its high standard.

In doing so they displayed one of the golden rules of communicating with pitch curators. That is, never reveal the truth, for fear the wicket may be worse next time or even better if your side has batted and has to bowl the next week. There is no greater insult to a pitch curator than to say they have prepared a poor wicket.

Despite this sensitivity, there are some groundsmen who you can say anything to and only receive a bemused shrug in response. These are the groundsmen who normally drive out of the car park at 4:21 pm with a smile on their faces.

Then there are the eccentrics. Former Lord Mayor of Brisbane Clem Jones was one of the better known ones. He was the curator at the Gabba when thunderstorms jeopardised the first day of the opening Test of the 1974-75 Ashes series. Despite the heavy downpours on the match eve, Jones made the most of a soggy mess of mud and grass, working with his staff through the night to ensure the pitch was ready for the first ball. It was later revealed Jones hadn't even worked out the pitch's position until the morning of the Test and was forced to use half of the wicket used in a Shield match two weeks before.

There are few pitch curators as well known as Adelaide Oval's Les Burdett. Now a regular on the speaker's circuit, Burdett became the youngest ever to prepare a Test wicket at the age of just twenty seven. He's seen as the world's best and is called on by cricket associations around the globe for his curatorial skills. Having worked at Adelaide Oval for forty years Burdett's also had a say in the ground's latest developments; the Sir Donald Bradman Stand and the Chappell and Clem Hill stands. He's even been awarded a Medal of the Order of Australia for his services to cricket.

It wasn't that long ago most cricketers played on concrete or matting pitches. Dad told me he never played on a turf wicket. Growing up in Adelaide in the 1940s and playing parkland cricket, he was just happy if the outfield was mown and didn't have too many grass seeds in it to cling to his socks.

For those old enough to remember World Series Cricket, they'll recall when car keys and a cricket pitch became inextricably linked, courtesy of Tony Greig's television pitch reports on Channel Nine. Greig would stick his keys into the wicket to gauge the moisture. I am not sure how Greig worked out how the pitch would play when he was captain of England, but I'm sure it wasn't by sticking a key into the pitch surface. There was also the 'player comfort' level related to the weather. Resembling a thermometer, the measure missed some key factors including the standard of the opposition and the state of the pitch. I'm sure Greig's comfort level was far worse when he played the West Indies' four pronged pace attack, regardless of how hot it was.

Pitches and curators have their own chapter in cricket history. The wicket at Old Trafford in the Ashes series of 1956 was so dry and conducive to spin it helped England off-spinner Jim Laker take 19 wickets in the one match. His spinning team mate Tony Lock, despite bowling as well as Laker, managed just one wicket. There is a famous picture of the groundsmen sweeping away the dust as the Australians prepare to follow on. In the shot, the staff looks like they are caught in the middle of a sandstorm.

A year earlier at Melbourne, Frank Tyson destroyed

Australia's batting line-up, bowling at a pace probably unseen since Harold Larwood's in the Bodyline Series in 1932-33. The cracks in the pitch made it look like the epicentre of an earthquake. In a sense it was. Tyson took 28 wickets for the series and the Ashes stayed with the visitors.

In the history of poor pitches, a single word takes on a meaning for Australian cricket fans. If you mention *Fusarium*, a dejected look will soon follow. It is the name of a fungal disease that suddenly appeared on the centre square at Leeds during the 1972 Ashes series. To say it was conducive to spin is like saying that Bradman could bat a bit. As Greg Chappell later revealed on the ABC television documentary *Cricket in the '70s*, this strain of the disease surprisingly struck the twenty-two yards of the pitch and nothing else. Its appearance came after Bob Massie's remarkable debut and inclusion in the record books. The series had been perilously placed at one-all after Massie's swing bowling bedazzled England's batting line-up, taking 16 wickets at the Lord's Test. The Leeds pitch changed all that. Derek Underwood, England's left arm orthodox spinner who was known as 'deadly' for his ability to exploit the conditions, was selected for the first time in the series. Underwood made the ball turn and bounce, making the Australians look as inept as England had in the preceding match. England won the match by nine wickets and retained the Ashes.

But when pitches are spoken about, Headingley 1975 provides the most disappointing reminder. We waited expectantly for the final day's play to be broadcast live on television. This was a rare event, but the level of interest justified the ABC's decision to take the satellite feed. Rick McCosker was on the verge of his first Test century (95 not out) as Australia were 3-220, chasing the target of 444. It promised to be a tantalising final day's play.

Just before the game was to start word came through. The

pitch had been damaged using knives and oil as part of a political protest against the conviction and jailing of armed robber George Davis, and it was beyond repair. The game was abandoned. Instead of watching McCosker make his way to a hundred and Australia reach an unlikely target, the only footage was of Ian Chappell wearing thongs looking like he had had a big night out (which he had) and Tony Greig dressed in a suit kneeling down to examine the pitch. A photo of the two captains was splashed across the front pages the next day and became the defining image of the match.

As it transpired, the heavens opened and it rained for most of the day, so little play would have been possible. This was no consolation for McCosker, just five runs short of the milestone all batsmen dream of. Davis was eventually freed but ended up in jail again after admitting to two other armed robberies, making a mockery of those who had supported him. There was some justice though. In the next Test, the final of the series, McCosker scored a hundred (127).

The pitches in major centres of Australia traditionally represent more than just the twenty-two yards of turf. They could be used to reflect the lifestyle of their cities. Perth was fast and bouncy; Sydney turned a lot; Melbourne, unpredictable; Adelaide tended to be flat and lifeless; Brisbane seamed early but was good once you were in. Like the cities, the pitches have changed, and like political parties are all a bit homogenous now.

As a cricket fan, I used to take part in 'pitch invasions' all the time. As a child of the 1970s, I ran onto the Adelaide Oval and stood on the pitch after each Test. In the frenzy of the final day sprint to the middle, my friends and I would try and souvenir parts of the pitch before the ground staff put on the overnight covers. Often there were small bits of dirt from the pitch that had shaken loose, but not always.

I once pocketed part of the pitch and buried it in the

backyard near our family's dinghy. It was late January in 1975. Australia had just demolished the hapless England. The day before, I stayed back after the game and watched Dennis Amiss, who had just scored a pair of ducks, wander out of the dressing room carrying his cricket coffin. He looked like he was in a state of shock. Just moments after the match finished I stood for a few moments at the northern end of the pitch, wondering what it was like facing Thommo and Lillee. Despite the mystical qualities of Test cricket, I realised they played on the same size cricket pitch as the rest of us. Working quickly, I used my pen to dig out a piece of the pitch from a good length that contained a ball mark. No one seemed to notice how deep I had to dig to dislodge it. That was apart from old Arthur Lance. He was the ground's curator whose picture I'd seen in the paper before the game. He gave me a stern look but I soon left with my memento in my pocket.

When I returned home I cleared some grass around our backyard pitch and planted the new piece of turf, despite concerns that it would become lost in the general foliage of the sturdy buffalo grass. When bowling later, I tried to land the ball on my part of the Adelaide Oval. The pitch, I had learned, was central to everything that happened on the cricket field. Just over twenty metres of turf is the critical hand when cricket's history is written. It pays to be respectful of it and those who prepare it.

Chapter 6

Where's Wally?

When you think of sporting heroes it's normally the big names that stand out. For me it was different. I liked players whose records were less obvious or at least in the developing stage. When I was in primary school my hero was Wally Edwards, even before he was picked for Australia. He was a left hander who batted with style. A poor man's Graham Pollock, if you will.

As it turned out he was a very poor man's Pollock, not that I knew it at the time. He finished his career with just 25 first-class matches under his belt, playing over five disjointed summers. The apex of his brief time in the spotlight was three personally unsuccessful Test matches in the Ashes series of 1974-75. Sadly Edwards wasn't able to take advantage of his team mates' confidence and momentum as they charged to a 4-1 defeat of the hapless tourists. Edwards's Test career was modest. In six innings his highest score was 30. I almost cried when Tony Greig got him for a duck in the second innings of the third Test at Melbourne. He'd made his top score in the first innings and looked like a Test cricketer. After the second innings disappointment, Edwards was dropped from the team, never to return.

My admiration for Edwards as a cricketer was simple. I loved the way he struck the ball. It was graceful and controlled. When he hit the ball it seemed to gain speed like a tennis ball carried away by the surf during a game of beach cricket.

I first heard about Wally Edwards when he scored a big hundred against the MCC for Western Australia. A picture of him at the nets, kneeling with one pad on and the other lying on the ground, caught my imagination. In the photo his grin looked like that of a teenager who had just asked his sweetheart out on a first date. Edwards had just been picked for Australia. It was only his second season of first class cricket and the idea of walking into an Australian dressing room with the likes of the Chappell brothers must have seemed intimidating.

He was from a land far away, Western Australia. To me Perth was an exotic land fertile with cricketing talent, which added to Edwards's mystery. Whenever I saw pictures of the WACA ground (the sound of the name was always a great source of humour to anyone hearing it for the first time) there was often a strong wind blowing that I now know as the Fremantle Doctor. Western Australia was like a different country. Two hours behind most of Australia, they would still be playing cricket there (in daylight) after *Countdown* had finished on a Sunday night.

When people asked me why Edwards was my favourite player I used to say 'because he was different'. All these years later this is still probably the best answer I can give. Perhaps it was his left-handedness that stood out. Maybe his long hair and casual manner reminded me of my older brothers. I was a right-handed batsman, but that didn't matter, I could have a left-handed hero.

In grade six when I batted I became an amalgam of Edwards and Ian Chappell. I shuffled across the crease like the Australian captain when I opened the batting on Linden

Park's chalked concrete pitch. But like Edwards I stood at the non-striker's end, chewing lazily on my gum like one of those old fashioned newspaper sellers.

In the Australian team that summer, my new hero was the new kid on the block. His name, Wally, even sounded different from all the others. I imagined his name on the side of a worn brown bookmaker's bag at the races. Wally Edwards: it had a resonance to it. Even for an eleven year old.

With the first Test of the Ashes series that year falling in November, memories of school and Test cricket are invariably intertwined. On the first day of the Ashes series I asked my teacher Miss Thompson, a blonde woman in her thirties, if we could watch the opening overs of the Brisbane Test. Luckily for me Miss Thompson was a sports fanatic. She had once asked me whether the England dual international Arthur Milton had ever played a Test in Australia. She knew I loved cricket and that my middle name was Milton. (I answered 'yes' to her question, although I didn't know who Arthur Milton was.) She also told me she once went out to dinner with the West Indian opener Roy Fredericks. It is all in the photo; Miss Thompson and Fredericks grinning over a glass of wine. She was also a Sturt football supporter who kept a scrapbook full of newspaper clippings from the club's golden era in the 1960s. This was the first time I had seen a preview where the players' heads were stuck onto an oval.

As the first ball of the opening Test of the summer approached, news filtered through that Australia had won the toss and were batting. In those days predicting the winner of an Ashes battle was harder. Miss Thompson tuned the TV as the black and white picture flickered in and out of view. The group of students had grown to twenty with several watching simply to avoid doing schoolwork. They were the ones who spoke over the commentary. When the recess bell rang, however, they quickly left, leaving only the hard core.

It was raining outside. As the milk bottles with their silvery tops arrived they made a clattering sound in their metal tray. Inevitably one bottle would not survive the ride and be found smashed, still in the tray or on the asphalt outside. As students scrambled for the milk, the Australian openers were seen on the television walking out to bat. A hazy reception became clearer as the tall figure of Bob Willis came into view. Suddenly Norman May's voice echoed around our transportable classroom. May and his co-commentators discussed the state of the pitch. A thunderstorm two days before the match had turned the centre square into a mud patch. Somehow, by the time the first ball was bowled, the mud heap had been transformed into a cricket pitch. They would talk about Clem Jones for years to come.

Then, the moment I had been waiting for. The Australian opening pair of Wally Edwards and Ian Redpath appeared. After some nervous anticipation, Edwards got off the mark with a flashing cover – a big relief for me. No one else at school appeared to appreciate the significance. Looking back the scene from the television returns quickly: Willis's huge run, the Gabba dog track decorated with flowers, people without shirts, an overcast day, Englishmen with a spring in their step.

Then came an early shock; Edwards was out, caught. Amiss took the catch on the deep fine leg boundary, threw the ball up and caught it again. It seemed a brave shot at the time, perhaps an instance where the ball got a little big on Edwards. Looking back at the footage now reveals more. It looks like a panicky slog.

The Australian captain Ian Chappell made his usual squinting walk to the middle and then a shuffle across the crease to get off the mark with a customary push behind square. Redpath was soon skittled with stumps flying everywhere and the Australians were two for ten. Miss Thompson, probably eager to head to the staffroom for a cup of tea, called out and we all had to go outside and play. My walk to the row of trees hosting games of cricket was slower than usual. On the school oval there was plenty of distraction from thinking about failed heroes.

The afternoon was punctuated by scores written on the blackboard, just under the homework box. I rushed the cycle home, hoping to watch the remaining play on the television. When I got home, I dumped my schoolbag under the kitchen table near the dog. A sandwich made by Mum and the news that Ian Chappell had just been dismissed for 90 in the long afternoon shadows of the Gabba provided a mix of emotions.

Australia was dismissed not long after I was home following Saturday morning cricket the next day. I can't remember how I went but I do recall the stoush between Tony Greig and Dennis Lillee which involved Australia's opening bowler being bounced out. Lillee and Australia's tangled-footed swing bowler, Max Walker, frustrated England's bowlers, adding 28 runs before Greig decided to bounce the tail out.

Perhaps Greig was unaware as to the extent of Lillee's successful recovery from a back injury. Most of us were. As Lillee angrily walked off the ground he almost collided with the England all-rounder, sending a message that was soon to become obvious.

That afternoon Lillee and Thomson began their blitzkrieg that continued for most of the summer. They intimidated and bullied England's batsmen with a blend of pace, aggression and fine fast bowling. The English looked like rabbits caught in a spotlight, all bar the lanky and arrogant Greig who struck arguably his finest Test hundred. Complete with his own signalling of boundaries, he used the upper cut to third man to perfection, angering and enthralling Australian fans at the same time.

Australia won easily but when we batted again, Edwards

managed only four to complete a double failure on debut. I was disappointed, but then remembered that just weeks before he had scored 153 against the MCC at Perth, the venue for the next Test match.

I saw every ball of the Perth Test from the hospital because of appendicitis. I couldn't eat a banana fritter for 25 years after vomiting all night. A mini TV in the corner of the hospital room provided solace for missing the last week of school with my friends. Edwards played, but only made 29 and 0. Australia won easily but I felt deflated.

The following Test was in Melbourne, where a crowd of 77,000 basked in Australia's dominance but went home unrewarded. Edwards retained his place, but did it again. He built me up in the first innings with a respectable score of 30, before falling for a duck in the second innings. I wondered why he would put me through such disappointment.

My fears were soon realised when Edwards was dropped and replaced by the heavy-scoring New South Welshman Rick McCosker. It got worse when McCosker batted like a Test veteran, negotiating the overcast seaming condition suited to the English bowlers and scoring a convincing 79 before a packed Sydney audience. The crowd of more than 50,000 were hemmed in with nowhere to look but the middle of the cauldron. A photograph of the Hill could have been a throwback to a famous picture showing Clarrie Grimmett bowling Frank Woolley in the Sydney Test of 1924-25.

The morning McCosker made his debut Dad and I searched the local shopping centre for a cricket cap in the school's colours. The cap was maroon coloured and more baseball style than baggy green but it was furnished with the letters LPCC (Linden Park Cricket Club), which of course didn't actually exist.

I was glad when McCosker was off the mark with a clip through forward square leg on the move. But not so happy when he cemented his place with such authority.

There was a brief chance of an Edwards recall when McCosker was hit in the head fielding at short leg. This was extinguished when the team for the Adelaide Test was chosen, with McCosker retaining the spot. By then Edwards was having trouble scoring runs for Western Australia. At school it was a matter of, 'Who is your favourite player now, Barry?'

Despite the usual fickleness of fandom, my interest in Edwards did not wane. The next season the West Indies toured and Edwards seemed as far removed from the Australian selectors' eyes as I was opening the batting for Linden Park under 12s. That year a new teacher at school, the future Australian captain Kim Hughes, was my cricket coach. He was from Western Australia and a former team mate of Edwards.

When WA played at Adelaide Oval, Hughes took my autograph book to the visitor's dressing room. When he returned it to school the names in my book included Dennis Lillee, Rod Marsh, Ross Edwards and John Inverarity. Those names, while valued, weren't as important as the signature of Wally Edwards.

At the end of the summer of 1975 I bought a magazine summarising the Test series. Edward's name was not even included. It was the final insult.

Twenty years later at the Adelaide Oval in 1996, I watched South Australia fight it out for a draw against Western Australia to win the Sheffield Shield. Gilchrist made a big hundred and displayed the beginnings of the explosive batting talent that would later emerge on the international stage. As I stood with my old school friend Richard Moody, watching his brother Tom lead WA, a tall bespectacled man walked over to say hello. I didn't recognise him. Richard introduced him; it was Wally Edwards, by then a state selector. We spoke about the game and then he moved on. I didn't have the heart to tell him he was my childhood hero.

Chapter 7

Cricket Fans, Writers & Books

Cricket and literature have fitted snugly together since the game began to flourish in the middle and upper classes of England in the nineteenth century. Thousands of cricket books were produced in the next hundred years, paving the way for the modern day phenomena of a constant stream of biographies and observations in a quantity unmatched by most other sports.

The extent of this excess was such that thirty Ashes related books were published in 2007 prior to Steve Harmison's embarrassing wide to open the series. Despite the 5-0 whitewash that Australia gave England, there was plenty of analysis, including Harmison's own version of events along with Australia's Justin Langer in their *Ashes Frontline*. (Harmison, who appeared to write his 'war diary' months after the events described, later revealed he hadn't even read his own book, which probably best sums it up.)

England and Australia contests tend to dominate cricket literature, although I suspect this will change when writers from the subcontinent gain greater acknowledgment. I don't know how many books have been written about the India-Pakistan rivalry. Not as many as the Ashes if my book collection is anything to go by. I have only a handful of books written by sub continental authors, including what I believe is the most informative and entertaining cricket tour book: *Pundits from Pakistan* by Rahul Bhattacharya, covering India's tour of Pakistan in 2004. The cricketing history between the nations is shorter and more interrupted than Anglo-Australian encounters. Yet the troubled political dynamic between the countries has bred a rivalry that few can match.

Cricket's connection to literature dates back a long way. The Melbourne Cricket Club library has French references to the game from the 17th century, while the first full description of a cricket match appeared in a Latin poem in Cambridge in 1706. There is also a strong association between great writers and the game. Nobel prize-winning author Samuel Beckett played first class cricket for Dublin University, but sadly wrote little if anything about the game. Others include James Joyce, Harold Pinter and Sir Arthur Conan Doyle – the latter of whom played first class cricket – although they also rarely chose to write about cricket.

This is different from distinguished writers in other countries and in particular the United States. Stephen J Gould's collection of essays on baseball, *Triumphs and Tragedies in Mudsville.* and Doris Kearns Goodwin's memoir about growing up as a Brooklyn Dodgers fan, *Wait till Next Year,* rank as some of the best writing about sport I have read. As does New Zealand author Lloyd Jones's *The Book of Fame* on the All Blacks 1905 tour of the northern hemisphere, written as a cross between a poem and a diary. Indian writer Ramachandra Guha's *Corner of a Foreign Field* illustrated his country's complex and at times turbulent relationship with cricket and reveals much about the game as the force driving social change.

In Australia, sports writing is not valued in literary circles. Fortunately that hasn't stopped the likes of Gideon Haigh, Martin Flanagan, Geoffrey Blainey and Brian Matthews from writing about sport at length. Cricket traditionally has been well served by quality writers dating back to 'Felix' – the pen name for former Australian player Tom Horan – and including Jack Fingleton, Ray Robinson and more recently Mike Coward.

Cricket has spawned many a book – in fact so many it's often been speculated upon as to why. American sports writer George Plimpton, when describing baseball's vast library, had a simple explanation: 'The smaller the ball, the more formidable the literature.' Golf with its rich canon of books would also confirm this.

Perhaps a more obvious reason for the large number of cricket books dates back to the mid-to-late 1800s when English public schools began their push for a 'sound body and sound mind'. Sport was considered character building and the perfect preparation for the military. It also meant that educated sons of the upper class, who were able to afford books, were raised on a staple of sport. Cricket among other sports provided centrepieces for *Boys Own Annuals* and featured in popular fiction of the day including Charles Dickens's *The Pickwick Papers* and Thomas Hughes's *Tom Brown's Schooldays*. A new genre was born and exploited.

There are several connections between cricket and books. Watching cricket can be a bit like reading a novel. Events unravel slowly, often like a journey, and sometimes in an unexpected way. Cricket's nuanced nature adds an edge to its intensity, attracting deeper analysis. As a game it has an unusual trait: players are judged on how they perform as individuals yet play as part of a team. This helps create circumstances where human character is more easily revealed. Cricket is embedded in the culture of countries it occupies, often providing a mirror to society.

Of course when there are books there are also collectors. This is a sub-set of cricket fans who speak in a language of their own. Editions of *Wisden Cricketers' Almanack* are discussed in reverent tones, (you can expect to pay over fourteen thousand dollars for a 1916 edition). Collectors come from all backgrounds and like any obsessive can be blind to quality. For some cricket book hoarders it's a matter of 'write it and they will come' (to paraphrase Kevin Costner in *Field of Dreams*). My own collection's inclusion of Glenn McGrath's *World Cup Diary* and Tim May's 'factional' account of an Australian tour of the subcontinent, *Mayhem*, is proof.

A cricket book collection just happens. You don't choose it, it chooses you. Collectors are reminded of the first step of the journey each time they stumble across their first book at home or on one of those many visits to second hand bookstores. My first book was Ian Chappell's *Tigers among the Lions*, which detailed the 1972 Ashes tour. When I read it now, I see it as a simplistic one-dimensional account, albeit of a significant moment in modern Australian cricket history. It appealed because it was written by one of my favourite players, Ian Chappell, and there was also a striking picture of Dennis Lillee on the cover, leaping before delivering the ball. Lillee's image is almost incandescent, set against the strangely green cover. Black and white pictures appear in unlikely places in the book, including one where Lillee is bowling a tennis ball at his former West Australian team mate Graham McKenzie, then playing for Leicester. The ball looks like a mini comet that's just missing the batsman's head. The story behind the joke also provided me with some insight into the larrikin spirit of the Australians.

Cricket provided much of my early reading experiences. Sometimes the appeal of a book was simply the photos which took me to another place. RS Whitington's *An Illustrated*

History of Australian Cricket was one I discovered in a boutique bookstore near our local deli. Finding the book was like discovering a lost treasure. It stood out because of its size and the striking black cover featuring a picture of Victor Trumper jumping out to hit the ball. It looked important. Big yellow letters were inscribed across its title, but the sealers for me were the photo of Ian Chappell on the back cover driving a ball, as well as a large number of black and white photos of old players I had never heard of.

Unfortunately, when I discovered the book I was ten years old and its price and placement in the store made it out of reach. But that didn't matter. Each time I visited the shop I asked the store owner to bring it down for me to read.

'Are you going to get your parents to buy you that book?' he asked one day.

I told him it was on my Christmas wish list.

'Let's hope Santa likes cricket.'

Christmas duly arrived and so did the big black book. I took time to carefully turn the pages and smell the freshness of the printed page, knowing I didn't have to return it this time. One of the pictures I hadn't noticed in my increasingly frantic bookstore readings was a famous painting of an imagined Test match at Lord's from the 1900s. It depicts a man fielding the ball on the boundary while in the foreground an attractive young woman sits in among spectators with big eyes staring out wistfully. It was as if she was trying to get a message out. The woman is actress Lillie Langtry, who was a lover of Albert Edward, the Prince of Wales. A less attractive face dominates the book's early pages: WG Grace, the grand old man from Gloucester. He looked anything but a cricketer with his long beard and unflattering frame. (Our son Ambrose has the initials WG in his name. I'm sure he'll see the humour in it one day.)

Collectors also have different ways of storing their books.

I've got a decent sized cricket library but I've never been obsessively driven to catalogue them in an order that has meaning. Unlike the angst-ridden character in Nick Hornby's *High Fidelity* – about the love life of a record store owner – I have no idea where individual books sit in my collection. I do however know where and when I purchased certain books. I can recall in specific detail where I was when I first read Gideon Haigh's writing. The book was *The Cricket War*, a look back at the World Series Cricket Revolution. Immediately I knew I had discovered something different. *The Cricket War* opened with Ian Chappell describing Australia's opening batsman Ian Davis, who was nervously adjusting his thigh pad before heading out to open the batting against the West Indies. Haigh's style was one I hadn't heard before and it brought the moment alive. It was as if I was suddenly taken into the dressing room and mind of the young opening batsman.

Cricket has its share of fascinating characters who are book lovers. Former Melbourne solicitor and music aficionado J Neville Turner is one. Neville's a Lancastrian with a great cricketing knowledge. Fluent in a number of languages, he's seen more than two hundred Test matches in numerous continents. His first was England playing the West Indies in 1957. It was the series spin twins Sonny Ramadhin and Alf Valentine bowled together, romanticised in *Wondrous Oblivion*, a movie about the struggles of Caribbean immigrants to England. Neville's also written about his World Cup soccer experiences, highlighting the valuable role of scalpers. He refers to them as great philanthropists of society who have helped him see a hundred World Cup finals.

Among cricket book collectors the question inevitably arises. What are you favourite books? It's always a difficult task and, for some, like having to choose between which of your children you'd like to spend time with. Bernard

Whimpress raised the topic of the best Australian (authored) cricket books in his quarterly journal *Baggy Green Journal of Australian Cricket*, a publication that provides a voice for those who like to write about the game.

Here is what I came up with.

1. Gideon Haigh's *Mystery Spinner*, about a life unexplored and exemplar in how to write a biography where information is hard to find. The back alleys and side streets of the biography are revealed as is a subtle study of personality. The reader learns about the psychological challenges placed on Test cricketers and the effect it can have on those of fragile temperament. It's a masterpiece and sheds light on a lesser known cricketer (Jack Iverson) for modern day fans.

2. Ray Webster's *First Class Cricket in Australia* (volumes one and two) gives a window into many detailed aspects of the domestic and international game as played in Australia, and is without doubt the most important cricket history resource. One of the joys of the book is that it tells you not only about the game but also offers snapshots of parts of Australian history. It has succinct descriptions and a great index of first class cricketers of the period.

3. David Frith's *Bodyline Autopsy*, for the author's ability to pull together so many parts of a complex story about one of the most significant moments in Australia's cricket history and still relate it in a way that's accessible for all. Short of a séance involving the Don, Jack Fingleton, Douglas Jardine and Harold Larwood, this is the definitive account of the most documented Test series in the history of the game.

4. Ray Robinson's *On Top Down Under* is beautifully told and gives meaning to the lives of those who have captained Australia. Robinson had an ability as a writer to shed light on the personal side of Australian cricketers, giving insights into what it was about them as people that made them behave and play in the way they did. In it Robinson adheres to CLR

James's famous maxim: 'What do they know of cricket who only cricket know?'

5. Mike Coward's *Beyond the Bazaar* is critical, for it traces a moment when Australian cricket matured, becoming more embracing of cricket in a region which holds the future of the game in its hands. Coward writes in a descriptive manner while not losing sight of the facts. As cricket in the sub-continent becomes more and more central to the game's control, this book will gain greater importance. It also marks a landmark change in the approach from Australian cricket authorities to travelling and playing in the region.

6. Christian Ryan's *Golden Boy: Kim Hughes and the bad old days of Australian cricket* is a brilliant account of Australian cricket in the 1970s and '80s, viewed through the prism of Kim Hughes's career. Without access to the subject and other major influences of the era, Ryan has skilfully woven together a narrative in a compelling and enlightening manner. After reading this you won't look at Hughes, Marsh or Lillee in the same way.

Then there were a host that almost made the cut:

Pageant of Cricket provides a pictorial passage through the game's mainly Anglo-centric eyes for the first hundred or so years. Pick a page – any page – and it should keep you entertained for a while.

Mark Ray's *Cricket Masala* also gets a tick for his look at the game and its followers in the sub-continent, a region that until recently was rarely reported on in Australia.

The Bradman Albums gives a glimpse of cricket through more than twenty years, beautifully presented, and a snapshot of the life of a player who dominated a game like no one else will.

Likewise, Jack Fingleton's *Cricket Crisis* and *Brightly Fades the Don* deserve a mention for views on the game and some of its most significant series from a former player and political journalist. Fingleton's insider's view of the Bodyline series and jaundiced observations of Bradman's personality are some of the most revealing of the era.

Haigh's *The Summer Game* tells the fascinating story of an under-analysed period of Australian cricket (1949-1971) that was crucial in understanding the genesis of World Series Cricket; the key moment that shaped the modern game. The same author's ability to bring the players and events of World Series Cricket to life in *The Cricket War* provides a great example of how to write entertaining modern history.

Frith's *The Ross Gregory Story* works with the idea of telling a story with the help of wartime letters. I didn't think it would work, but it's a credit to Frith's story telling abilities and empathy for his subject. It reveals much about life as a wartime pilot and sporting hero.

Given the resurgence of the Ashes campaigns, Hart and Whimpress's *Test Eleven* gets a nod for most underrated book and one that places the matches in a historical and social context in a way that is engaging for readers of all tastes.

Greg Chappell's *Successful Cricket* is for the coaches. The pictures tell the story simply as to how to develop technique. Why don't coaching books nowadays have such detailed illustrations of the fundamentals of the game?

Greg Growden's *A Wayward Genius: the Fleetwood-Smith Story* and Adrian McGregor's *Greg Chappell* are probably the best cricket biographies apart from *Mystery Spinner*. They give insight into the thinking behind two vastly different cricketers and men and the way they lived their lives. Growden's book importantly highlights the fragility of some who make it to the top in his story about arguably Australia's most enigmatic Test player.

Growden's *Jack Fingleton: The Man Who Stood Up To Bradman* is also worth a look to gain an insight into the insecurities that drove Fingleton not only as a player but also as a man and critic.

Jim Young's *Any Old Eleven*, which shows life as a park cricketer, must be the favourite of any of the books that goes to the village green or parklands to sample life. Anyone who's ever played, bowled a ball in anger or experienced the pressure to not give your team mates out LBW despite a vociferous appeal will relate and enjoy this book.

Charles Davis's *Test Cricket in Australia 1877-2002* is again a record of Test cricket and the circumstances in which matches and series were played out. It is detailed, informative, easy to interpret.

The debate about the best cricket books will continue. One thing that appears certain is that Gideon Haigh, the man who writes cricket books quicker than most of us read them, will continue to feature on the best of list.

Chapter 8

Walters' Mitty: Doug Walters's Last Ball Six

'Doug Walters on 97; here's the last ball of the day's play.

He's hit it... it could be four.

A six... a six it is.

What a fantastic finish to one of the greatest days you will see in Test cricket.'

Norman May, ABC cricket commentator, December 14, 1974.

It wasn't 'gold, gold, and gold' – Norman May's famous Olympic Games call as the Australian men's swimming team charged to a gold medal at the 1980 Moscow Olympics – but it was pretty close. Doug Walters's six off the last ball of the day brought up a hundred in a session in an Ashes Test, and in terms of defining events in cricket, was the equivalent of that gold medal.

It's a moment a lot of us remember. Some of us were mowing our grandparents' lawn, others listening in the car as we drove to summer holiday destinations. Many were, like me, in front of a television. When Walters nonchalantly smashed Bob Willis over the WACA boundary, I was 11 years old, sitting on a beanbag at my friend's house watching on a small black and white television.

'He's not going to make it,' said Tauny, a 21-year-old medical student who we paid attention to. His comment seemed reasonable. Walters looked uneasy in the last over, pushing and prodding. Needing seven to reach his hundred, he looked uncertain as to whether to pursue three figures that night or wait until the next day.

When the final over began, Ross Edwards was on strike, and then a leg bye opened up the possibility of Walters and history neatly merging. (They were eight ball overs in those days.) An uninspiring top edge moved Walters to just three away from a hundred, but then he stalled again. Three balls remained and three runs were needed. The second last delivery found Walters clumsily playing back, considering a single then stopping.

Then it happened; Willis stormed in, hair bouncing everywhere. He dropped the ball short, and Walters leant back and pulled it over the boundary. At my friend's house we all jumped up from our beanbags and cheered. We watched Willis despondently collect his sweater from the umpire as other players sprinted toward the dressing room.

It added to the joy that Bob Willis was on the receiving end. The tall and lanky quick was the anti-hero for the Aussie fans. He conveyed little personality, spoke in monotone and rarely smiled. His movements on the field were jerky. When he batted he looked like a robot whose power supply was intermittently disconnected. For Australian cricket fans it would have only been better if Tony Greig was the bowler.

The fact that it was Walters punishing the English bowlers also gave the moment another edge. He was the player we all loved. Slightly balding, he seemed to have the self-deprecating nature of a country farmer who played cricket for fun. Walters struck a chord with fans because he appeared to

Another four for Walters , Perth 1974-75.

represent what we believe to be quintessentially Australian traits: bush bred, laconic, talented, and not one to be sucked in by the hype and bullshit (even from his team mates!). It looked like cricket was something he played when he wasn't having a fag or beer. I couldn't have imagined him in a day job. Most Australian men could identify with him. He was in a sense one of us. It was just that he could bat.

Walters was in some ways the odd one out of Chappell's band of aggressive and arrogant Australians. There was of course an appeal to the Australian side's hubris and success with more than 250,000 people attending the Melbourne Test that summer. (Enormous gate receipts from England's visit helped further open the eyes of the players and business tycoon Kerry Packer to the value of the game. The World Series Cricket revolution was a heartbeat away.)

Walters was exciting to watch. He had one batting speed and that was quick. Everything about his stroke play was spectacular. In our quieter moments we imagined ourselves doing what he did in Perth. When Walters was on-song he made batting look easy, like we could in our dreams. His pre-match batting session, so it was said, consisted of tapping the ball a few times up and down on a horizontal bat and saying, 'That's it; I'm hitting the ball well.' Maybe this was only in England, where he struggled on the seaming wickets. His failures only endeared him to us more.

When Walters made 'that stroke', he'd dared the cricketing Gods and won. Using a high risk tactic, he bisected two fieldsmen, burying the ball deep into the crowd off the final ball of the day. It was a hundred we didn't expect, or at least not that night, not even from Dougie. Walters liked to do things in his own time and his own way. He executed the stroke with such ease that when he followed through he simply continued walking to pavilion. He walked while others ran, until it became obvious he was about to be swamped by the crowd. It was the only time Walters looked slightly ruffled.

Photographer Patrick Eagar captured it all perfectly. Despite the ferocity of his stroke, Walters's follow-through is balanced and graceful. The sense of drama is accentuated by the bowler's long shadow falling across the pitch. Willis is captured following through and balancing on his left foot. He still has a look of hope on his face, perhaps believing that one of the two fieldsmen positioned deep on the leg side might catch the ball. It's an expression that soon changed. The non-striker Edwards has a combination of a smile and a grimace on his face as he backs up with his bat in his left hand.

He also scored a century (115) in that innings; it was Edwards's only Test hundred in Australia yet few remember it. It's a bit like Arthur Morris batting with Bradman in his final Test match. No one remembers Morris's 196, with Bradman's second ball duck providing the pivotal moment in history.

Walters's century at Perth appealed to our romantic side

but it also had statistical importance. He reached the milestone from 115 balls in a session, helping Australia to score 351 in 76 overs that day. It was his second century in a session in eighteen months. More than 22,000 were at the ground to see it (although like the first Tied Test in Brisbane, many more have claimed they were there).

After great excitement there is often anticlimax and so it was with Walters. He was caught at slip early on the third day without adding to his score. It didn't take the gloss off the innings that led to the creation of the 'Doug Walters Stand' on the Sydney Hill for the fourth Test of the series. The 'stand' consisted of a white sheet with Walters name on it. It shone among the vast sea of faces crammed into the Sydney Cricket Ground. Many turned up just to see Walters bat. He was out for one and five.

I had my own look at Walters in the Adelaide Test. Sitting among a crowd of more than 30,000 at Adelaide Oval, I watched him take on a rampant Derek Underwood, who made the most of the damp pitch and dark skies, consistently turning the ball square and with considerable bounce.

Australia slumped to five for 84 in its first innings as Walters counterattacked, scoring 55. It provided the foundation of Australia's eventual total of 304. By the close Underwood had taken seven Australian wickets with an unlikely contribution from hometown hero, leg-spinner Terry Jenner, who managed a career best of 74.

But it was Walters who swept Underwood aside with a canny ability to hit across the spin. One shot over mid-wicket looked like an effortless clip off his toes and brought the crowd to its feet. In its execution Walters snapped his heels together, springing his body into the stroke, legs straightening as he struck the ball. Walters's innings was a lesson in how to bat on a difficult wicket against a world class bowler. It was one of several he provided that summer.

Chapter 9

World Cup Final 1975: a Night to Remember

The picture – lodged in the memory like a first girlfriend – is of bespectacled and near exhausted West Indian captain Clive Lloyd holding the silver Prudential trophy high above his head in the fading light at Lord's. Windies wicket-keeper Deryck Murray is one of the players in various states of exhaustion captured in the background. The Duke of Edinburgh, having just presented the first ever cricketing World Cup, stands by with a look of bewilderment on his face.

It is a simple photo that tells a complex story. The World Cup final marked the moment when one-day cricket officially arrived on the international scene. It also signalled the emergence of the West Indies as a cricketing force that was on the cusp of dominating the world scene for close to two decades.

The idea of a world cricket championship had been on the agenda of the International Cricket Conference for some years. One-day cricket provided a solution that was manageable and able to be fitted into the Test calendar. Limited overs cricket was played in the county competition in England from 1963 and in the Australia domestic competition from 1969, yet six years later only eighteen internationals had been played, and those mainly in England.

The World Cup was an anomaly, set in the middle of an oddly abbreviated four-Test Ashes series. Three years later, Kerry Packer's World Series Cricket provided the limited overs game with momentum via night games and coloured clothing, yet it was the 1975 World Cup and in particular the final, that opened the door enough for cricket fans around the world to notice.

The inaugural World Cup was only distinguishable from its current form in the details. Matches were 60 overs, played in daylight, with no fielding restrictions or coloured clothing. That first championship was over in two weeks, unlike the 2007 competition in the West Indies that stretched over 42 days.

In 1975 there were only six Test-playing nations making up the international cricketing scene. Test matches had been long dominated by England and Australia, with some success from the West Indies. India and Pakistan played well at home, but often struggled overseas. New Zealand, despite having been part of the international scene for more than forty years, was considered a fledgling side. The apartheid regime in South Africa had ruled it out of official competition and Sri Lanka had yet to achieve Test status (but was included in the World Cup). Zimbabwe was then Rhodesia and provided players for the East Africa team at the competition, while Bangladesh was not yet on the world cricketing radar.

Nowadays the World Cup attracts enormous media interest, yet thirty years ago it barely raised a whisper in Australia, especially in the competition's opening days. The first chapter of World Cup '75 couldn't have been more disappointing for organisers. India's Sunil Gavaskar thumbed his nose at the event by batting for 60 overs for 36 not out in the sun-drenched opener at Lord's. Chasing England's 334, India managed 132 for 3 in what was an absurd display of limited overs batting. India's supporters agreed, with a few even running out to the middle to remonstrate.

There were more surprises from Sri Lanka, who performed well against Australia, with some of its top order batsmen suffering some heavy blows from the extreme pace of Jeff Thomson. They fell short of the target of 328, losing just four wickets for 276, but had made a clear statement in their first outing in elite company. Alan Turner, who later provided the smiling backdrop for cricket's first streaker at Lord's, scored Australia's first one-day hundred. (Despite his habit of having a back lift that drifted toward leg slip.)

Then there was little West-Indian Alvin Kallicharran, who bludgeoned Dennis Lillee around the Oval during a match-winning innings of 78 against Australia. At one stage he harvested 35 runs off ten balls from Lillee. His fourteen boundaries and a six in a partnership of 130 with Roy Fredericks made Australia's total of 192 look like child's play.

But not all the matches fell the way of the West Indies. They were lucky to be in the finals at all. An unlikely one-wicket win against Pakistan helped them scrape through. No thoughts of match fixing back then when the Windies scrambled home after being 64 runs in arrears with only two wickets in hand.

When Australia reached the semi-finals, the local media suddenly became more interested. One image defines Australia's win against England. Rod Marsh is in full stretch leaping to his right in front of Ian Chappell at first slip. You can see the ball in his glove as he catches Tony Greig off Gary Gilmour.

It was one of Gilmour's six wickets for 14 as he derailed the host country, leaving it stumbling and staggering to a total of 93. Overcast skies helped Gilmour make the most of Headingley's green top, reviving memories of Bob Massie's 16 wicket haul at Lord's three years earlier. The home crowd moved from a state of shock to delirium as Australia followed suit, struggling at 6-39 before Gilmour combined with Doug Walters to guide their side through to the final. It was a see-sawing contest that clearly overshadowed the West Indies' five-wicket win over New Zealand in the other semi-final. Again it was Kallicharran who breezed his way to 72 to help the Windies cruise past the Kiwis' total of 158.

And so it was to be a world championship between the established power and the emerging one. The limited coverage of the tournament was forgotten when we discovered the final was being broadcast live on ABC television.

The night of the final was a rare one in our household. My parents went out together dressed in black tie in what turned out to be their last formal function together. They divorced 12 months later. My teenage brothers were also out for the night. There would be no discussion about whether or not I could watch the cricket; it was just me, our dog Snoopy and the black and white television.

Once the house had emptied, I watched the start of the telecast with excitement. It grew with the sight of the two West Indian opening batsmen, Gordon Greenidge and Roy Fredericks, walking out to open the innings. Dennis Lillee measured his long run as the Lord's Pavilion hummed with anticipation. Spectators hurriedly took their seats. Twelve thousand miles away the electric heater warmed the chilled air of our lounge room. The sound coming from a crowd of animated West Indians was colourful. Parts of the crowd resembled London's Notting Hill Festival. Many were shirtless but had enough headwear for a fashion parade. Some were seated inside the small pickets behind the white ropes that lined the boundary.

Then all of a sudden it was on; the final began.

Fredericks hooked the first ball of the second over from Lillee for six over the fine leg boundary. The West Indies' crowd began its cacophony of noise with bells and whistles before falling silent. Mysteriously, Fredericks started walking off with the look of someone who had just been given a parking ticket. He had tipped off the leg bail with his left foot as he followed through and was out, hit wicket.

Enter Australia's nemesis from their loss against the West Indies at the Oval, Kallicharran. He struck two crisp cover drives off Gilmour, but surprisingly he was gone soon after, caught behind nervously jumping and prodding at a ball outside off stump. The force of the competition was teetering at 2-27.

Greenidge not only looked strange in his blue terry towelling hat but a little overawed. He was subdued, scoring just 13 in eighteen overs and when he edged Thomson to Marsh, the West Indies were 3-50.

Slow going it may have been, but the crowd provided its own entertainment. The final's carnival atmosphere was highlighted by supporters mixing with the Australian fieldsmen on the boundary. Max Walker joined in and exchanged hats with a London 'Bobby' beneath the scoreboard near Lord's Father Time.

The West Indies were struggling but no-one bothered to tell the skipper who walked languidly to the middle. On Lloyd's arrival the game's tempo changed. He stood and delivered, while Rohan Kanhai nudged and deflected. So patient was the veteran that at one stage he went scoreless for eleven straight overs. By the 36-over mark the West Indies had made 149. The contest was on, helped by the Aussies uncharacteristically dropping catches, including Lloyd at 26.

Decades later I listened to a tape of English commentator John Arlott. It sounded just like it happened yesterday. Semi-final hero Gilmour took some severe blows. Arlott observed, 'Gilmour, my word, how life can change between Wednesday and Saturday.' Lloyd's casual slow tapping of the bat as he prepared was misleading. He looked like a giant with long arms, scattering the Australian bowlers and fieldsman to every corner of Lord's with his lusty hitting. 'You must believe me that there is no Australian within shouting distance of Marsh,' Arlott continued.

It didn't matter the onslaught intensified, as did the lyrical commentary:

'This game is just sailing out ahead of Australia like an express train leaving the station,' Arlott declared, and, 'Umpire Bird is having a wonderful time signalling everything in the world including a stop to traffic coming on from the High Street.' I now wonder what it must have been like for Arlott's fellow commentators when he was in such form. Perhaps a little like Australian players batting with Bradman.

When the broadcast stopped because of a break in the satellite feed, the frenetic nature of the West Indies crowd could still be heard on the small radio I found in my upstairs bedroom. 'There's Lloyd's hundred … and the whole crowd seething with leaping West Indian delight … I can only say it was worth this: I thought I saw a policeman applauding…'

Then success. Lloyd was caught down the leg side by Marsh. Gilmour had the final say and despite the treatment he received, he was the only bowler to take five wickets for the match. He took 5-48 after twelve long overs. Lloyd's 102 consumed 84 balls and saw him leave the ground to a standing ovation. A consultation between umpires Tom Spencer and 'Dicky' Bird about the validity of the dismissal angered part of the Calypso crowd. They needn't have worried; the party has just begun.

Kanhai eventually went for 55 in his final innings for the West Indies. He had reminded us of his greatness. Hard-hitting cameos of 36 from all-rounder Keith Boyce, and an undefeated 26 from Bernard Julien helped the West Indies to a score of 291.

An unbeatable total? Not according to Arlott: 'At the end of the innings, 291 for 8. I would think this was an impossible total if I didn't know Australians.'

When the innings closed I was still awake on the couch. Back from their night out, Mum retired to bed while Dad briefly watched on as Australia batted. They soon lost McCosker for seven and I was again left alone. Some hope followed; Ian Chappell and Alan Turner took the score past 80. Then Viv Richards pounced, with a direct hit on the stumps to run out Turner who, after propping and sprinting, was caught just short of his ground.

The Chappells then accelerated the scoring rate, with 26 from four overs. At tea, Australia was 2-107 from 25 overs. The clock in our dining room ticked over to 2:30am. I couldn't remember ever having been up this late and the house was silent apart from the willow trees blowing in the winter winds. Soon I was asleep.

But the game marched on. The Chappells put on 32 then Greg Chappell went. Run out. Richards again swooped after confusion between the batsmen. He repeated the favour with Ian and Australia slumped to 5-170. The West Indian crowd intermittently ran onto the ground. When Gilmour was caught on the boundary for 14, Kanhai was almost mugged by over-exuberant supporters.

Suddenly I was awakened by the sound of the television test pattern. It was almost light outside as I made my way upstairs to my bedroom. It was all over. I didn't know the result but by then I didn't care; I was exhausted.

At breakfast Dad greeted me with the score: Australia had lost. Just. The news that night showed the final confused and comical scenes. Australia's fast bowling duo Lillee and

Thomson scamper frantically between the wickets after a no ball, a catch and a crowd invasion. A few balls later the game ends when Thomson is run out wandering down the crease trying to hit the ball out of the suburb of St John's Wood. Australia lost by 17 runs. At the end the umpires and players frantically ran to a roped off area of Lord's as a sea of exuberant spectators approached.

The first World Cup was over and cricketing life as we knew it had changed forever.

Clive Lloyd's West Indians take the spoils,
World Cup Final, Lords, 1975.

Chapter 10

Christmas in Whites

1976: Australian vs Pakistan at Adelaidc Oval

Coming as it does in the middle of the Australian summer, Christmas has a stronger link with cricket than merely the chance of getting a new bat. There is also now the 'tradition' of the Boxing Day Test Match, which began in 1981-82 with a Test against the West Indies with less than 40,000 turning up to watch day one.

Some cricket fans look forward to the match more than Christmas itself. The game is the talking point around festive recoveries across the country. Many who can't make it to the ground park themselves in front of the television for hours on end. The first day's play normally attracts the largest Test match crowd of the Australian summer.

Before the Boxing day tradition was established Sheffield Shield matches between South Australia and Queensland were played on Christmas Day at Adelaide Oval. (Oddly SA officials initially wouldn't agree to play Shield cricket on Sundays but allowed a Christmas day match – except for when it fell on a Sunday.) The tradition of the December 25th match stretched from 1926-27 to 1969-70. Key state rivals Victoria and New South Wales also developed a tradition of Boxing Day contests.

Only two Test matches have been played on Christmas Day. They were both in Adelaide against the West Indies in 1951-52 (day three) and India 1967-68 (day two). Nine years later in 1976, when Australia played Pakistan in a Test, it began on Christmas Eve with a rest day the next day. It was the only time I sang carols to my neighbours. Quaint as well was the long forgotten rest day. Nowadays there's just not enough time to fit one into crammed international cricket calendars. Why have a day off when you can schedule another financially lucrative one-day match?

Players must have looked forward to the Adelaide Test for the rest day alone. Part of the occasion was lavish foods and wine mixed in with tennis at the Yalumba Estate at Angaston in the Barossa Valley. The estate was owned by Wyndham Hill-Smith, Clem Hill's nephew, who played nine games for WA in the early 1930s. But these were the days when touring sides played against state teams as well as country elevens as they traversed the country in a much more leisurely fashion. Cricket fans came to know and appreciate the visitors. In 1960-61 the West Indies discovered just how much when Frank Worrell's side was farewelled by half a million Melburnians in a motorcade.

In the summer of the 1976-77 the constants of the cricket season were starting to change. That year the Adelaide match was the first of a three-Test series against Pakistan. It marked the start of an unusually scheduled international cricket summer. By mid-March Australia had played sides at home and abroad. After drawing against Pakistan, Australia had the better of New Zealand in a two-Test series away before accounting for England in the enthralling Centenary

Test. It was almost a visit to cricket's future.

The Adelaide Test had personal landmarks for me. It was the first time I went to Adelaide Oval on my own. It was also the beginning of a routine, including a visit to the Oval nets to watch the players practise the day before the match. Pre-match sessions then consisted of nets, basic fielding drills and catching practice using the slips cradle. It was all pretty straightforward and not particularly demanding compared to what happens nowadays.

The players hurriedly walked down the back steps of the dressing room past the vines that climbed the rear wall of the Members stand. The asphalt path running next to the lawn tennis courts and cafeteria was strewn with autograph collectors who they did their best to avoid. I was more interested in ensuring my position behind the nets provided a clear line of sight. The day before the match I watched Australia's opening batsman Ian Davis bat against the gentle medium pace of Doug Walters. Davis had been recalled to the Australian squad after he scored hundreds against Victoria and South Australia. A lot was riding on his comeback Test after managing just 143 runs in nine innings, all against New Zealand.

Nicknamed the 'Wizard' because of his prodigious talent as a teenager, Davis wasn't living up to his reputation that day. Only 24, he looked young enough to be at high school despite a hint of facial hair resembling a moustache. Walters as usual was bowling line and length but snail-like in pace compared to the speed of Thomson and Lillee. (When they bowled, even off just a few paces, the net behind the batsman broke back suddenly when the ball hit like a sheet on the clothesline in a storm). That day Davis was bowled at least six times in a ten-minute batting session, all by Walters. The flat and hard turf wicket of the Adelaide Oval nets played perfectly. When Davis walked out of the net, Walters gave his team mate a friendly smile and ruffled his hair.

The first day of the Test was uncharacteristically overcast and muggy. Only eleven thousand attended, with Christmas shoppers making the most of the last minute opportunity to stock up on presents. On the first morning I was sitting beside the player's gate, close enough to notice the different shades of green in the captains' blazers, when Greg Chappell and Mushtaq Mohammad walked out to toss the coin.

Pakistan won the toss and batted, at first slowly. Debut opener Mudassar Nazar began nervously but survived the early storm from Australia's pace trio of Lillee, Thomson and Gilmour. On 13, Mudassar was caught on the crease groping at a ball outside off stump. Marsh did the rest. The Pakistani batsmen played differently, using wristier strokes. Their top batsman Zaheer Abbas played with such an open blade at times it was as if he only hit balls square on the offside.

Then immediately after lunch it happened: a miscued pull from Zaheer. Somehow Thomson and the short leg fieldsman Alan Turner zeroed in on each other in search of the ball. As they moved slowly and obliviously toward one another the crowd released a high-pitched sound. It was like a car crash, in slow motion. We all expected one of the fieldsmen to pull out and for the other to emerge triumphant with the ball. Zaheer started walking off, shaking his head and annoyed at his miscalculation. Then there was the collision and a loud crunch.

Thomson and Turner lay motionless on the ground. Australian fielders and the umpires rushed to their side. Turner stirred first then Thomson, who looked in serious trouble. All he could do was hold his shoulder. The man with Herculean talents looked helpless. Surprisingly Turner emerged relatively unscathed and continued playing. For Thomson it was the turning point of his career. As a bowler he was never the same again.

The collision put a dampener on the whole day. The pic-

Collision course, Thomson and Turner, Adelaide Oval, 1976.

tures of the Australian pace man bandaged up in hospital sitting with his beautiful blonde wife the next day did little to allay cricket fans' concerns.

As it was, Pakistan's middle order struggled to take advantage of Thomson's absence. When Asif Iqbal was dismissed for a duck courtesy of Kerry O'Keeffe's straight leg spin, the crowd made its largest sound for the day. Departing at 152 for five, Asif looked glum beneath his big white sunhat.

That day I saw Javed Miandad bat for the first time. Just two months earlier he scored 163 on debut against New Zealand and backed it up with 206 in the same series. One of Javed's team mates ran onto the field and took his photo when he walked out to bat. The teenager made only 15 before being bowled after batting for almost an hour. He showed enough with a style that day more centred on deflection than power. By stumps Pakistan was all out for 272. It looked easily gettable.

After the rest day, Australia batted. Davis surprised us all by scoring his first and only Test hundred. Davis played with a poise and confidence he'd lacked previously, bringing up his century by pulling a short ball from Saleem Altaf over the midwicket fence into the Victor Richardson Gates for six. He modestly celebrated then tugged his cap and marked his crease as if to settle for another long innings. It wasn't to be, dismissed for 106, but his Test career was rejuvenated. That night Walters was unbeaten on 33 on his way to his second and final Test century at Adelaide.

Pakistan set off 182 runs behind, but without the prospect of facing Thomson, whose accommodation had changed from a city hotel to Wakefield Hospital. Zaheer, who had a reputation for being a little brittle against pace, took advantage, scoring 101 to mark an impressive double. The second innings also proved more fruitful for Asif Iqbal, who helped number eleven batsman Iqbal Qasim add an unlikely 87 during an undefeated stand of 152. Australia's tactic of placing the field deep had played Asif back into form.

An hour into the final day it looked set for a tantalising finish. Australia needed 285 in around five hours on a wearing wicket. It began badly. Davis was bowled for a duck off the third ball of the innings by Sarfraz. He was back to his nets' form. Half centuries from Greg Chappell and Walters helped Australia to within 66 runs of a win with five wickets still in hand. Two quick wickets fell and then Gilmour, having been rushed up the order, failed. Then Marsh and the adopted home town hero Gary Cosier did the unthinkable and blocked their way to stumps, causing the normally docile Adelaide Members to jeer. Even from a kid's point of view the response looked pathetic.

Australia finished the day at 6-261, just 15 runs short of the target. Marsh and Cosier had batted as if the pitch were a minefield. As the crowd left, the suited-up press men banged their fingers down hard on typewriters as if expressing their opinions in frustrated tones. The next day the sports pages were full of vitriol and photos of Marsh and Cosier leaning forward, heads over the ball as they played defensive dead-bat shots. The match deserved a better ending.

Chapter 11

The Magic of Linseed Oil

Some smells take you straight back to childhood. For me it's the combined wood and varnish aroma of linseed oil. Knowledge about the oil was something fathers passed on to their sons. We learned it was an important substance if you wanted your bat to last. At our home the oil resembled other liquids in Dad's shed, but was different. Its container glistened with a yellowing tint and workman-like look.

Derived from the seeds of the flax plant, linseed oil was applied in two ways. You could stand the bat in a saucer of oil overnight, allowing time for the fluid to make its way up the blade. There was a small hole at the very bottom of the bat where the oil entered. Getting the smell out of the saucer could be a problem, but this was usually the least of concerns for young cricketers with a new bat. (Parents tended to have a different view.) The alternative and more common approach was to gently massage both sides of the bat with a cloth. You made sure to spread the oil evenly across the blade's surface, including the edges and sometimes even the back of the bat. It then had to be left to dry overnight before it could be used.

You didn't just oil a bat once. It was ongoing. If you were oiling an older bat it was best to clean it to ensure the 'cherries' or red marks on the edges were removed. Cleaning your bat was like purging the bad strokes from your repertoire. There was an art to oiling a bat and using an unclean rag was to be avoided, with the aim being to make the bat sparkle. The way a person looked after their bat told me a lot about their attitude toward the game. Neglect came in many forms, but none worse than allowing it to be ruined by rain. When it rained I would wipe my bat on my cricket whites, although Mum didn't appreciate it.

Nowadays when I visit a friend's or an acquaintance's house I usually seek out their bookcase to see what they're reading. It's my barometer for understanding where they're coming from or what phase of life they're at. When I was young I would look at their cricket bat to see whether they had the symptoms of dryness, chipping around the edges and flakiness on the front of the blade. Neglect was easy to pick. You could even hear it in the sound the bat made when it hit the ball.

To me owning a cricket bat was a special privilege and you benefited from the runs it help provide. In turn, it needed constant maintenance in summer and kind storage in the winter. Nestled among the footy boots and jumpers my bat took on a lonely unwanted appearance when cricket season ended. It went into hibernation, often hidden in a cover.

When it came to caring for your bat, one of the dilemmas was whether to use it against composition or 'compo' cricket balls. These were plastic-like with a white seam and had the hardness of a brick. 'Compos' were much cheaper than leather case balls but had a reputation for causing the most pain if they hit you on the thigh or on the palm of your hand. In the class structure of cricket balls, 'compos' were at the bottom of the pile and ruined bats, especially those not oiled properly. Few of us could afford leather cricket balls so it became a matter of using a 'compo' or a tennis ball. Using a tennis ball outside of the school grounds was for those who didn't take the game seriously. In the primary school Saturday morning competition, the 'compo' was the standard match ball. The dilemma presented itself: use your own bat and see its life reduced but increase the likelihood of a successful season. The alternative was to take your chances with a bat from the kit which was often falling apart and invariably about two sizes too big. They were usually bought with a 'one size fits all' mentality and kept in the back of teachers' cars with the rest of the sorry-looking kits items, like pink protectors with cracks in them.

It wasn't uncommon for some kids to go through an entire season using a kit bat. They would often then wonder why they couldn't hit the ball off the centre square. I used my own bat, much to the surprise of my friends, who then assumed I didn't mind it being ruined and so they asked to borrow it when I got out.

Nowadays technology has moved on and many bats come pre-oiled and protected by a cover. The skill of applying linseed oil to a bat and nurturing the blade will soon be lost like the trade of a blacksmith. Boundaries may be easier to hit with today's technologically enhanced bats, but there's nothing quite like the smell of oil and softened wood that immediately follows. Even if it was against a 'compo' and you knew you'd have to do it all again soon after.

Chapter 12

A Big Day Out and Memories of Bob Woolmer

Bob Woolmer is dead. I heard it on the radio, along with reports of his hotel room with blood on the walls, the day after Pakistan suffered its shock loss to Ireland at the World Cup in the West Indies. The final image of Woolmer I saw was of a forlorn man resigned to surrendering. It was captured just after his side's surprising defeat at the hands of the tournament minnows, Ireland. Rumours about his death swirled for months after Jamaican Police declared it would be the subject of a murder investigation. There was talk of match fixing when the Pakistani team was placed under suspicion. Some even called for the championship to be abandoned. The murder investigation was later withdrawn but the circumstances surrounding his death even now remain unclear.

Woolmer is the second player from the 1977 Centenary Test who has died. The first was the youngest: David Hookes, after a bar-room altercation. Gary Gilmour could easily have joined them if it wasn't for a last minute liver transplant which saved his life. Woolmer's death, like Hookes's, took from the game a coach who had much to offer. Thinking about them both takes me back to World Series Cricket and Football Park on a forty-degree day when cheating the school system to watch a cricket match seemed a priority.

It's November 1977. Woolmer is playing for the World Eleven against the West Indies at Football Park. I'm in the middle of my year nine exams, and this is the first time Kerry Packer's WSC had made it to Adelaide. My first week of exams finished around lunchtime and an operation that had been planned well in advance was about to swing into action.

Peppy, my opening batting partner in the school under-14 team, and I had decided to abscond from school to see the action live. He had the nickname because Peppy was the first of us who could grow a moustache like the ethnic kids could. Other friends who might have been game enough to make the journey were doing a French exam at the time. I am still good friends with them, though to this day I have yet to hear them utter a word of French.

The covert operation required catching the bus from the Parade outside our school grounds to West Lakes and then on to Football Park. For two teenagers unfamiliar with public transport it was a major challenge and one that had to be timed to perfection. We realised that suspicion would be raised if we loitered too long at the bus stop, so we made the break from school in much the same manner that we ran between the wickets – with a sense of panic.

The bus arrived on time and as it made its way into North Terrace we realised nothing would stop us. Our sense of freedom grew at each bus exchange. When we arrived we also discovered the cost of watching the best players in the world was half the price of entry into Adelaide Oval to see

South Australia play against India.

The heat was extreme in the concrete surrounds of Football Park. The sun reflected off the aluminium seats, making the glare in some parts of the ground unbearable. Sitting in the open outer was a test of our endurance, or stupidity. I can't even remember if we wore hats. We soon sheltered in the stand where it was cooler but still suffocating. In the outer some brave people sat under umbrellas. Cameramen sitting on temporary metal platforms looked drained. There appeared to be more Channel Nine employees than spectators. Cricket's establishment must have been laughing.

The game lacked atmosphere, which didn't fit with the high-powered adverts we'd seen on television. The crowd was tiny, totalling just hundreds. It wasn't at all like going to the footy and must have reminded the players of their club days. Any applause echoed around the ground, highlighting the stadium's emptiness. Players moved slowly around the field.

The West Indies were bowling. 'Big Bird', Joel Garner, all six foot eight inches of him, stood at gully, towering over everyone. He moved in between overs like a giant. When he bowled he lumbered to the crease in such a way that all his movements seemed to be exaggerated, with his extremities catching up with the rest of his body by the time he released the ball.

There wasn't much action so we wandered through the grandstand with a sense of adventure. We walked through to the level where the players were sitting. During the tea break the pin-up boy of the Australian side, David Hookes, strolled by. Hookes was playing for the World team that day, perhaps in a vain attempt to attract a larger local crowd. He appeared taller in real life, and was wearing thongs that made a loud clicking sound on the concrete surface as he walked by. When we looked over he was busy clearing out food from his teeth and seemed bored.

Out the back Dennis Lillee was bowling to Rod Marsh in a basic net that was set up. Lillee was bowling off a few paces, but the ball skidded and jumped from the matting pitch at great speed. Marsh batted on instinct. We stayed, hoping we might see one of the Chappells practising. They never showed up.

Not long after tea we were debating whether to leave when we saw Bob Woolmer and Zaheer Abbas practising. There was no one else around. We watched as they threw balls to one another. Woolmer, speaking in his plum English accent, asked if we would like to throw some balls at them.

So there we were Peppy and I, throwing balls at these world-class players. They told us where to throw so that they could practise certain shots. Zaheer wanted balls thrown short and wide of the off stump, while Woolmer practised his driving. It was embarrassing when we threw it too wide. We spent about fifteen minutes with each of the players. Occasionally Peppy and I would look over at each other in amazement about what was happening. Our bragging rights to our schoolmates had grown. The day could now be defined as a success.

Afterwards Woolmer and Abbas took us into the World team dressing room, and gave us a drink. They also introduced us to Tony Greig who said hello but not much more. The room itself was a haven from the heat with all the cricket gear scattered around. The other players were next door. I don't remember asking for an autograph; perhaps we were both still in a state of shock.

Years later when I heard of Woolmer's death, my reaction was a different type of shock. I thought back and realised I had only seen him bat in a match on television. That was when Woolmer scored his two tons against the Australians in England in 1975. Then in his debut season of international cricket, he nudged and deflected his way to big scores, including 149 not out.

I also watched him open the batting in the Centenary Test after the Australians were bowled out for 110. He was out just as the shadows began to close in on the MCG. He made only 12. When Woolmer walked off the ground a camera close-up highlighted the Lions badge on his England cap.

Chapter 13

Playing Away: Cricket in England

It's ten degrees and pissing down with rain. I look at my wet and dirty pads. My hair is soaked and my nose has a large water droplet hanging from it. My short-sleeved jumper is weighed down heavily with rain. I resemble someone who's just emerged from the bottom of a footy pack. I'm playing cricket in England. It's not quite the sun-drenched village green scene I had imagined.

I look at my Australian mate, Graham, at the non-striker's end. He has that superior look of a batsman who is set. 'I think it's time for the long-sleeved jumper,' he says.

'Either that or time to get out,' I respond.

It's a sentiment I unintentionally follow through with, by spooning the ball back to the bowler.

'Soft,' says Graham.

As I walk past the bowler's end more relieved than disappointed, I tell Graham I'll keep him a place at the table for afternoon tea. The assortment of cakes and sandwiches at tea in England is often a wide-ranging and sumptuous affair. Even our club, Ashford in Middlesex, half an hour out of London, far surpasses the selection of plain (read stale) biscuits I'd been accustomed to in Australia. I haven't been in England long but know that the not-out batsmen often miss out on the spoils. Some of us are known to start taking our pads off before we have left the ground to limit the delay to the tea room.

A little wet and cold it may have been, but playing cricket in England is an adventure hundreds of young Australians, often those playing various levels of club cricket, experience. It is as much a personal journey as it is about sport. A select few play as professionals, mainly in the north of the country but most, like Graham and I, play for the love of it, and sometimes for board and lodgings.

The year I travelled was 1984, a landmark year for George Orwell but without Big Brother on our television. Margaret Thatcher was the Prime Minister and stories about miners striking in the north dominated the news. The Los Angeles Olympics were on the television, although the coverage didn't extend to Australians. That summer U2 walked further into the spotlight with their live album *Under a Blood Red Sky*. Walkmans were the iPods of the day but were the size of several modern-day mobile phones. If you were hip you wore a mullet hairstyle with a poofy bit at the front like the blokes from the English band Wham! (although none of us knew then they were gay). Frankie Goes to Hollywood's *Relax* and Nena's *99 Luftballons* were always on the radio. Like most of the blokes I played cricket with I was oblivious to the social and political messages about sex and Cold War tension.

We played for Ashford, which was in Middlesex, but competed in the Surrey Championship League, one of the strongest competitions in the south of the country. Cricket was taken seriously in the Saturday league, which occasionally featured first-class and former Test cricketers. Sundays were reserved for friendly matches that were more relaxed and provided a good chance to get some form back and eat a lot at afternoon tea.

We stayed with Arthur, a family court lawyer, who had a liking for bowling very slow medium pacers and complaining about Australians. Most weekends he'd disappear to the English countryside, supposedly to play village cricket. He gave us virtually free board for close to six months in his three-bedroom 1960s villa. It took a while to get used to the tiny backyard but the house was close to the centre of the town and he even had pay TV.

We all envied our team mate Chris, who worked for a major sports company. He was hung like a horse and had a drop-dead gorgeous blonde as a girlfriend who we'd see sitting in his flash sports car. He was also a handy cricketer and a charming bloke. Chris and his girlfriend travelled to the Los Angeles Olympics for work. We all wanted to be Chris.

Our new town was small but busy and close enough to Heathrow Airport to see a steady stream of traffic flying overhead. Ashford dates back to 1086, and rates a mention in Britain's oldest public record, the Doomsday Book, when it was named Exeford.

To a young Aussie bloke used to the open spaces of large backyards and the nearby sprawling Adelaide foothills, it took a while to adjust to the lack of general space. Traffic around the town was always busy and the planes from Heathrow added to the congestion. In the south of England it seemed that unless you lived in some palatial country house, open spaces were mainly experienced on the cricket field.

We played cricket on average three times a week. Finances were tight but helped out by part-time work on the club grounds. It was half an hour by train to London's Waterloo Station, where you would connect to the Underground, or the Tube as they called it. Crowds of people walked in waves through the tunnels beneath the road's surface as the continual 'Mind the Gap' echoed in your ears from the loudspeaker. I had never seen or heard anything like it. We visited St James Square, where young policewoman Yvonne Fletcher was shot dead and ten others injured at a small demonstration outside the Libyan People's Bureau. It had made the news in Australia the week before I left for England, making the experience of standing at the site where flowers were left a little like a dream.

I sought sanctuary from the noise at one of the major stretches of water down the road from where we lived. Yachts decorated the reservoir that seemed to stretch on forever. Ashford's neighbouring towns included Staines, now known as the setting for Ali G although to us the town represented one of the easy beats on the cricket field, while Sunbury was the closest main rival.

A lot of club members worked at Heathrow Airport or commuted to the Thames Valley or London to work. From our house it meant a walk down Ashford's main thoroughfare, Church Road, then veering left to the train station. In Ashford some police got around on bicycles while mini cars with three wheels were used mainly by older people.

When I arrived in May the weather was still cold, and overcast for days on end. It was unfamiliar territory. There was a multicultural mix of mainly Pakistanis and Indians in the local community that contrasted with Adelaide's social make-up. My daily visit to the corner store meant being met by a beautiful Pakistani girl who smiled flirtatiously while her father watched on. He would loom larger after I had bought the milk and papers, ensuring I didn't linger despite wanting to.

By June the sun came out and the days were long, with sunset well after 9pm. Cricket continued into the late evening in midsummer. Well before Twenty20 cricket appeared as the new frontier, it was seen on club grounds around England. It didn't happen much at Ashford but we filled in for other teams in mid-week twilight six-a-side matches. Fielding was exhausting, and made worse by the sledging from locals who watched from the sidelines, often with beer in hand.

Ashford's ground was then at Woodthorpe Road. It wasn't your quaint English village green, but rather a small neat oval hemmed in between houses. It was home to the type of scoreboard I had seen used at Test matches on the television, displaying the bare essentials such as the total, wickets down and player's scores. When bank loans, the threat of an injunction from flying cricket balls, plus the need for a larger space for cricket and hockey loomed, the club moved its ground near the Ashford Hospital, just off the Main London Road.

At times residents living next to the ground watched from their front yard before wandering over to the clubrooms after for a drink. One man, Ted Sutton, used to make the stumble back to his house each Saturday night at the same time. Some nights we would all gather outside the club to watch his circuitous return leg.

The club room at Ashford wasn't your typical rustic stand. It was a brick building with wire covering the windows to protect them from any lofted strokes. Surrounded by a school on one side and houses on the other, a massive net covered the fence at the scoreboard end. A small car park next to the change rooms seemed immune from cricket balls. Our club rarely practised, because there were so many games to be played. That was the official line anyhow.

We had our own umpire who travelled with the team. Dennis was an amiable man who officiated fairly. He got it right most of the time and he was so pleasant few of us ever took an issue with him over decisions we didn't agree with.

All the cricket – whether serious league cricket on Saturdays or the friendlies on Sunday – was one day cricket. If you won the toss, the batting side decided how many overs it would bat, unless they were bowled out. The captain usually declared after around 45 overs but this could be a lot longer if they thought they had no chance of bowling the opposition out. Winning the toss became doubly important. If you weren't all out and failed to reach the total, the match was drawn, unlike in Australian one-day games where you'd lose. It all seemed strange and uninspired. So many games petered out in a draw.

However, the cricket was much friendlier than in Australia, where you could be sledged for not walking to the crease properly. In England I was only ever sledged by fellow Australians, English players who'd spent time in Australia or the occasional South African.

We had a good mix of older and younger players. They turned out for far more years in England because of the shorter games and cooler conditions. In Australia, once you got into your 30s, spending long, hot Saturday afternoons on the cricket field became increasingly problematic, especially if you had a family. In England the club was more than somewhere where you just played cricket. It was a meeting place where a lot of kids grew up and families gathered, sometimes every night. The town church was nearby but it rarely attracted the numbers Ashford Cricket Club did.

The standard of cricket in the league was below A-grade district level at home, but moments were often of a higher standard. Wimbledon was the strongest team in our competition. Led by former England captain Freddie Brown's son, it included future New South Wales all-rounder Brad McNamara. It also had Simon Dyson, the best bowler in the competition. It was said if he hadn't chosen to be a solicitor he would have played cricket professionally. In an era when the leg-spinner was considered an ancient artefact, he terrorised us. Bowling off a few paces, he had a wrong'un nobody could pick. Our clash with the league leaders was one-sided, with most of us struggling against the wily skills of the solicitor-cum-leg spinning magician. We had even recruited NSW's Phil Marks, who'd played at Ashford the previous year, but he also failed, stumped charging carelessly down the wicket. I later batted against Australian spinners Peter Sleep and Tim May at the heights of their Test careers and neither compared with Dyson.

Considered the toffs of the Surrey Championship League, Wimbledon had a luxurious two story pavilion, turf practice wickets and several grounds. Not many club sides could get an annual financial bonus from one of the most famous tennis championships in the world. Each year the club leased out its grounds as a car park for the two-week Wimbledon championship and made a killing.

One of the highlights of the summer was against a Marylebone Cricket Club (MCC) side featuring three Sri Lankan Test players. Later that year Sidath Wettimuny, Ranjan Madugalle, and Asthantha de Mel helped Sri Lanka to challenge and eventually draw with England in a Test at Lord's.

As the MCC chased our 240, Wettimuny, who a month later scored 190 against England, gave a batting lesson on his way to a hundred. I helped him along the way. Though I'd been seen as a nets bowler at home, it was a different story in England. I was part of the attack, benefitting from the ball gripping on the softer wickets. I even occasionally turned one. I bowled the best I ever had in ten overs to Wettimuny. It made little difference. On average one ball per over was dispatched with the sweetest of timing to the boundary. It taught me the value of patience and showed how top players placed the ball with precision.

Madugalle didn't make many runs but showed signs of class and a demeanour which illustrated why he was called to Australia to smooth relations when tempers frayed in the 2007-08 Australia and India Test series. Sri Lanka's opening bowler de Mel was quick by club standards. He bowled with pace and skidded the ball off a lifeless wicket.

Acting as ambassadors on Sri Lanka's first Test tour of England was obviously a priority. The night of the MCC match, the Sri Lankan players, dressed formally in their blazers, mixed readily with us in the club bar for hours. When they played they also didn't act as if they owned the field, unlike some Australian Test players I later encountered in club cricket.

As one of the two overseas players at the club, expectations loomed large that I would play a role in helping Ashford win the championship. It didn't happen. The greater expectation was that you'd drink your fair share of beer. This did happen. Unlike in Australia where a duck or dropped catch saw you packing the kit, offenders had to buy the jugs of beer that were so much a part of the after-match socialising. Simply not drinking meant you had to shout a jug. I later learned just how important drinking was to the cricketing culture.

As the season progressed, the older players continually spoke about the club tour. Each year in June, Ashford sent a team down to Devon for a week's cricket on some of the most picturesque grounds in the country. It was a picture postcard tour that played sides at Budleigh Salterton, Torquay, Exeter, Sidmouth and Devon.

We travelled in our own cars in convoy along the motorways in the south of England and stayed at a hotel by the beach at Sidmouth. The grounds in the south were larger than the club grounds we played on in the Surrey Championship. Some were beautifully manicured with deckchairs scattered around the ground and scorecards of the match. It was the stereotypical English cricket scene I'd been missing. The ground at Sidmouth was the most scenic. It had a double storey pavilion and was surrounded by a series of croquet and bowling lawns on one side. From the grandstand you could see the ocean, which seemed to glisten all week.

Cricket was just one aspect of the tour. It was all a very social occasion. Post-match meals took place at various curry houses where fines were dispensed and various misdemeanours mentioned. One night our captain announced one of my slow-breaking off-spinners hit for six had actually reached the sea. He also emphasised that this was a beach paved with pebbles, adding greater weight to the fine. It was then increased further because it was the first time in the club's history a ball had made it to the waters of Sidmouth beach. (Graham was also fined for taking so long to find the ball.)

Traditionally players outside of the club were invited to tour. That year the guest players were the Zimbabwean-born Phil Marks and his Blues team mate Dave Gilbert. They were both rare talents. Marks, tall and blond, was built like an AFL player. He had an ability to dictate terms as a batsman that I had never seen before. He'd played for Ashford the previous season and dominated. (Subsequently any Australian playing for Ashford drew comparison, although Graham and I did our best to bring down expectations. From what the club said, we succeeded.) I always thought Marks would play for Australia. The closest he came was sub-fielding for Australia in a one-day final in the mid-1980s at the SCG. He even managed to take a spectacular catch on the boundary. A chronic back problem in the end limited his opportunities.

Gilbert was playing as a professional in the north. He generated enormous pace from a short run up and had an unnerving ability to skid the ball off a length so that it sailed past the batsmen head high. The next year he opened the bowling for Australia in the Test match at the Oval.

The cricket could be competitive, but it wasn't too serious. On tour some teams we played were made up of mainly middle-aged and older cricketers. It was generally these matches when I was brought on to bowl very early to try and boost the opposition's total. One team we played looked as if they had walked out of a retirement home. Appropriately called the Gentlemen of Devon, they were three for none after two overs. The balding grey-haired opening batsmen who charged Gilbert was thankfully dismissed before he was hit in the head. It was the only time I had been worried about a batsman's health other than my own. I was brought on for the third over.

Living in England taught me about the different cultures in the country. Ashford's 'fast' bowler was an Indian Sikh called Shammi, who challenged his parents' authority by dating non-Sikh women and drinking. He chewed vast amounts of gum to hide the smell of the post-match beers on his breath. There were no West Indians in the Ashford sides but there were plenty in the opposition, mainly tall quick opening

Ashford Cricket Club 1984 – Dennis Grey (umpire), Don Taylor, Bruce Cotton, Keith Bedford, Neil Smith, Graham Lewis, Barry Nicholls, Robert Evans, Tony Beckett, Graham Beckett. Front row: Gareth Evans, Peter Curzon, Jerry Tombleson, Chris Evans, Trefor Evans

bowlers.

Our team had a lot of characters. Don, the gruff detective, complained if the scoring rate ever went below four an over; needless to say he was particularly harsh on me. There was Neil, the young angst-ridden leg-spinner, whose father was also the groundsman and still insisted on preparing some wickets on the far side of the centre square just twenty-five metres from the boundary. Chris was the ever-reliable opening bat whose technique was unorthodox but very effective. Peter, a moustached, grumpy middle-aged off-spinner, had a habit of rubbing his hand on the pitch before he started a new over, just to make the batsman think he looked like he could spin the ball. (Sadly he could, but only marginally more than me.) Graham was an agile wicket keeper studying at university, who tended to choose his fixtures more carefully than most. His father, Don, a useful left arm orthodox, was an elder at the club and full of wit and wisdom.

Our skipper was Jerry Tombleson, a tall and solidly built all-rounder. He'd played district cricket in Newcastle and was more Australian than English. He was the laid back guy, the one that each club had who held the team together. He spent most of his life at the club bar as part of his 'Captain's Duties', a defence he often made to various girlfriends over time.

Perhaps the one who stood out the most was Bill, the club critic, who in his own terms was the side's spare part: the player who batted eleven, didn't bowl and was hidden in the field. 'Technique', Bill used to say, was English cricket's problem. The summer of 1984 was when England was whitewashed 5-0 at home by the West Indies and talk of the home side's performance dominated bar-room discussion. 'Talent' might have been the more obvious word for Bill to use when talking about the deficiencies in England's line-up, although they did convincingly defeat a weakened and unsettled Australian team 3-1 the next year.

Another of the pleasures of playing cricket in England was the quirkiness of some of the grounds. The Surrey League had Streatham, the equivalent of the Canterbury Oval in Kent where a tree sat within the boundary's perimeter. Playing against the London club Mitcham, which claims to be the oldest cricket club in the world, provided a unique experience. To walk onto the oval from the pavilion you had to cross a major road, which made waiting to bat an unsettling experience. Graham did me a favour by getting out in the first over for one of his rare failures, saving me a long wait surrounded by the cars and trucks. We were told of a game where commuters on a London bus stuck in a traffic jam once stood up and applauded a batsman bowled first ball.

I went to Lord's twice that summer. The first time was to watch the all-conquering West Indies take on England in the second Test of the series. I remember overcast skies, beer and cold pasties, a packed house and England making a game of it. England's left-handed opening batsmen Graeme Fowler scored his first Test century as the home side slumped from a respectable 2-167 to a modest 286.

Chris Broad debuted for England, scoring 55 and blunting the pace of Garner and Marshall, who peppered the batsmen with bouncers. As I sat on the grass near the boundary (in the same place I had seen West Indies spectators celebrate during the first ever World Cup final) I watched England's all-rounder Geoff Miller embarrassingly run out for a duck at the non-striker's end. He had turned the ball to deep fine leg before slowly wandering down the wicket for what he'd assumed was an easy single. As Miller strolled, Eldine Baptiste grabbed the ball and threw down the stumps. ('And it's good night to you, Mr Miller,' said Richie Benaud as the credits rolled on BBC's television highlights.) Mike Gatting's dual LBW dismissals while padding up to Marshall were almost as humiliating. I saw Gatting err in judgement in the first innings from high in the Members pavilion, where you could appreciate the sheer force behind the deliveries from the West Indian pace bowlers.

I missed the West Indies successful run chase of 342 in just 66 overs for the loss of one wicket. Gordon Greenidge scored an undefeated double century, but I wasn't there. I had a ticket for the final day's play but caught the wrong train back from Malvern. It was an express to Birmingham instead of London. I blame Dad. I'd spent the weekend staying at the hotel our family had lived in for six weeks almost twenty years before. The lesson I learned from the day was that when you are twenty-one it's time to start scrutinising train timetabling advice from your parents and not to listen to your Walkman as a train was departing.

I managed to hear the final stages of the Test at the train station at Oxford, where I stopped off on the return leg to make my way to London and then Ashford. Despite my frustrations, the brief wait on the railway station platform provided me with one of my most enduring memories of the trip with the hustle and bustle of students at the station departing for summer holidays. Many were talking about the exciting finish taking place at Lord's as they said farewells.

The second time I went to Lord's I saw Sri Lanka draw with a tired-looking England side after the visitors scored 491 in the first innings. The crowd was much smaller than it had been for the West Indies Test match but still had little to cheer about. This time I sat in what is now known as the Tavern Stand. Looking across at the Members the eight foot slope was much more obvious. Botham took six wickets as the game petered out to a draw. His speed and ability to hit the pitch hard seemed more penetrating than two years before when I saw him bowl for England in Australia.

One of Ashford's key rivals was Guilford, our closest neighbours. Set in a city, their home ground was a world apart in terms of facilities and so, it seemed, in the wealth of its members. In 1984 Guilford's overseas' player was a young all-rounder called Nick Foley. He went on to become a Victorian state squad member but sadly passed away in his 30s because of cancer. He stayed with the Guilford club president's family in a house that resembled a country manor. One of his team mates was the former England international Graham Roope. The middle order batsman was known at least in part in Australia for his stoic 77 against the Australians at the Oval almost ten years earlier. When he was dismissed the close-up picture of the stumps being spreadeagled provided the end shot for the television highlights.

No such image or score in Ashford's encounter with Roope. He was out third ball for a duck, caught top-edging the ball to backward square. It was the third innings for the gun recruit and his third duck. The only unfortunate element of the dismissal was that it wasn't me who delivered the long hop; it was our other off-spinner who used the scalp as evidence that he should always be called on to bowl first.

The big game of the year was the President's Eleven, where anyone who had anything to do with the club tended to congregate for the annual match. A three-course meal with wine and port was served and a betting tent set up, although there was no mention anywhere of odds of 500-1. Club President Dennis Cornwell bragged for weeks how this would be the strongest President's side in the club's history. He'd even recruited the wonder boy Phil Marks for the match, which had the atmosphere of a country fete. We chased down a sizable total of more than 250, with Graham scoring an unbeaten 150. We only lost one wicket on the way. The openers put on plenty before I had a hit. Graham hit the winning runs to finish off a day to remember.

Looking back, the surprise of the summer was that we played almost seventy matches in five months on all types of grounds from Edinburgh to the Isle of Wight. We learned how to drink warm English beer, eat roasted peanuts and chat up the local girls. But most of all we learnt about life beyond our own backyard.

Chapter 14

Looking for Kim Hughes

What was it about Kim Hughes that made so many of us fall in love with him and the way he played? He was a modern day marketer's dream: blond, good-looking, athletic, and talented. Also highly confident, he still displayed a boyish touch of vulnerability. In the late 1970s and early '80s, Hughes rode the crest of a cricketing wave before a catastrophic fall from grace. By the close of the 1980s, the golden-haired boy of the establishment was left for dead by Australia's cricketing administration. Mention Hughes's name to the younger generation of cricket fans and most won't recognise it. But for a legion of cricket supporters, Hughes played cricket with an assuredness we all wished we had. He played three of the most remarkable innings in the game's history, and was also among the first of a generation of players to adjust to the combined pressures of Test and one-day international cricket.

Australian captaincy arrived prematurely for Hughes, proving to be a poison chalice that contributed to the sudden and dramatic end of his Test career. History shows he was the wrong man at the wrong time in the wrong job. Hughes is now most remembered for crying when he resigned after another shattering defeat against the West Indies. But there is much more of his story to be told. The scheduling of Australia's international cricket commitments during the time in which Hughes played is revealing in itself.

The Australian Cricket Board, unable to resist the lucrative financial pulling power of the West Indies, scheduled series involving Australia in 1978, 1979-80, 1981-82, 1984 and 1984-85. Few batsmen withstood the dominance of the four-pronged West Indian attack without blemish. By the end of Hughes's career his batting average had slumped from 42 to 37 in the final two series alone. Batting under these conditions was hard enough, but the knock-out blow was provided by the burden of captaining a developing side that was divided in its support of the captain.

My own preference – some might say bias – is easily explained: I went to Linden Park Primary School, where Hughes taught in his first full time teaching commitment.

It was the summer holidays of 1974 when I heard my school had employed a teacher who played cricket for Western Australia. I doubted the news at first. Most of the teachers at school were far too old, probably in their 30s. They weren't young and athletic and they certainly weren't first-class cricketers.

But when the new school year approached, it was confirmed. Kim Hughes was going to teach at my school. I didn't know much about the new teacher's cricket career. I read he had been 12th man for Western Australia and soon found a picture of him in my collection of cricket magazines. It revealed Hughes had played for a club in Perth called Subiaco and was the youngest Australian to score an A-grade hundred. He'd made the score when he was 15, just three years older than I was at the time. Disappointment followed excitement as I discovered I was in the Open Unit classroom for the new school year and none of my teachers were called Hughes.

That summer, all the talk was whether Ian Chappell's dynamic team, which had been undefeated since its 1972 tour of England, could win back the Ashes. England was without its stars of the previous tour to Australia, Geoff Boycott and John Snow, but began the series as favourites. Australia's bowling quality was unknown. Dennis Lillee was returning from a crippling back injury and Jeff Thomson, whose Test career consisted of one match against Pakistan, had the unflattering figures of 0-110. Thomson bowled with a broken toe on debut, although we didn't know that at the time.

The summer of 1974-75 changed everything. Both bowlers intimidated the English batsmen with a hostile display that hadn't been seen since 'Typhoon' Tyson swept through the Australian batting line-up in 1954-55 with extreme pace. Such was the impact of Australia's pace duo in their first outing at the Gabba that the series was effectively over after the first Test. Australia won by 166 runs. The win was a significant one in cricketing terms but also a severe psychological blow to the entire English batting side. By the end of the season all the kids in our neighbourhood were trying to bowl fast, imitating Lillee's long run and Thommo's slinging bowling action. I tried as well, but realised my attempts at real pace were futile.

The long summer holiday consisted of watching cricket on television, nets sessions in the backyard, eating leftover fruitcake from Christmas lunch and playing cricket board games. All the excitement about the Ashes fuelled interest in the game and made the idea of a first-class cricketer at my school even more exciting.

I went to the Adelaide Test and was surprised at how far back the wicket keeper and slips stood when Lillee and Thomson were bowling. By the time the holidays ended England was on its way to its only Test win of the series. Thommo was injured and so was Lillee after he dispatched

England's strong hope Dennis Amiss for this third consecutive duck. England's beleaguered captain, Mike Denness, scored a big hundred as did the most despised of all English batsmen, the gnome, Keith Fletcher. But by then it didn't matter.

On the first day of school I saw Hughes walking to the staff room for his morning tea on what must have been his first day of teaching. He looked young and fit and moved quickly. There were no signs of the nerves that young teachers often had. I was jealous of those in his class, which was often outside playing continuous cricket. In the schoolyard rankings, this made Hughes a good teacher.

My teachers that year included an elderly lady with little interest in sport and a middle-aged man who told us he read encyclopaedias at home each night for entertainment. They promised us time playing games outside, but these rarely eventuated. There was always some kid who preferred not to head outside and would shirk on 'picking up papers responsibility', much to the chagrin of most of the class.

Life improved dramatically when I found out Hughes was the year-seven cricket coach. It was soon obvious he preferred centre wicket practice on the main oval to net sessions. Hughes worked out that I had trouble judging a run and helped with my calling between the wickets. One night he asked me to stay in the middle practising my calling 'loud enough so that the whole school could hear'. I continued calling out at the top of my voice despite the odd looks from passers-by. It was embarrassing, but the drill got the message across.

One night not long after practice finished, our year seven footy coach, Mr Hudson, bowled at Hughes on the concrete centre wicket. Hudson was the Ron Barassi of Linden Park Primary. He had long curly hair, a Chappell-like moustache, and wore flares and loud psychedelic shirts that revealed a healthy patch of chest hair. He was friendly but competitive and bowled off a long run, complete with Gordon Rorke drag and slinging action. He seemed quick to a twelve year old. This night he bounded up and bowled a hard red 'compo' at full pace at Hughes, who was batting without pads and with a harrow-sized bat. With little effort Hughes leant on the delivery and clipped it away to the mid-wicket boundary. The ball moved off the bat at a pace I had never seen before. It smashed against the metal fence before Hudson had finished his follow-through. My footy coach didn't bother bowling another ball.

Hughes emphasised the importance of fielding. He told us that it didn't matter how good we were at batting and bowling, we would still be expected to spend a long time in the field, so you may as well enjoy it. Previously our only fielding practice consisted of a batsman hitting catches to a group of fielders standing in a semicircle. That all changed with Hughes, who had us doing some unusual catching drills. Before we batted or bowled we had to try to underarm the ball past our team mate standing between two cones a metre or so apart. Short sharp catches on a one-to-one basis helped quicken our reflexes. When he showed us the activity he did it with such enthusiasm that he made the experience more like football practice. At times I wondered if we'd ever get a chance to bat.

The new coach also talked about the significance of being light on your feet and the value of knowing how to skip. Hughes skipped like a boxer, moving the rope around his body at lightning speed. He also spoke about the importance in batting of knowing how to play straight. Explaining batting in simple terms, he said it was simply a matter of copying the action of rocking a baby in the cradle and showed the movement of top and bottom hands working in unison. These cues made it much easier when I practised playing straight-bat shots in front of the mirror.

A gifted footballer, Hughes also helped out with our school footy team. He occasionally stayed behind after school to help kids who couldn't kick straight. He had an uncanny knack of kicking low screw punts and splitting the lunchtime players. Off his boot the ball seemed to travel like a low-flying missile.

First term came and went quickly. During the holidays I stood in the outer and watched Hughes play for East Torrens in the A-grade final at Adelaide Oval. The last time I had been there I was one of a crowd of thirty-five thousand cheering for the Australian team but now the ground was almost empty. The East Torrens' wickets tumbled quickly and Hughes continued his poor run as his side collapsed to be all out for around a hundred. Hughes scored less than 10 and batted without a hat on a dark and overcast day. It was strange to hear the echoes of the players celebrating on the field whenever a wicket fell.

He stayed on as a teacher at our school until the end of second term, then returned to his home state, aiming to break into the Western Australian team. That year was the last my family spent at our home in Lascelles Avenue. I had lived there for all of my primary school years and when my parents divorced I was just as concerned about losing my connection with the neighbourhood as I was about the breakdown of the family unit. By the time cricket season came around again, the only news I had had of Hughes was of him scoring a hundred for Western Australia on debut against New South Wales. His influence then, just a year on, suddenly seemed a long time ago.

Later that season he made a hundred against the touring West Indies side after scoring a golden duck in the first innings. In my first year at secondary school I saw a photo of Hughes wearing a kilt in an Australian cricket magazine. He had been playing league cricket in Scotland and had identified a family clan connection and scored a lot of runs. In a kilt he didn't look much like my old teacher.

In the summer holidays of 1976 I watched Hughes score a ton against the visiting Pakistan team on television while listening to a long-playing vinyl ABBA record, the one with the helicopter on the cover. The name of the album was *Arrival*, which accurately summed up Hughes's new stakes in the Australian cricket scene.

In a meteoric rise, Hughes was selected in the Test twelve to play against Pakistan in the Melbourne Test match. As twelfth man he ended up spending a lot of the time on the field because of an injury to a team mate. There was a crowd of almost fifty thousand on one of the days that Hughes was substituting. The newcomer got a very loud cheer from the crowd when he rolled backwards with the force of the ball when stopping an overthrow. He toured New Zealand with the Australian side near the end of that domestic season, but missed out on playing in the Centenary Test.

Instead David Hookes was picked to make his Test debut. Alan Turner, a tenacious left-handed opening batsman, made way for Hookes who had just completed a purple patch of five hundreds for his state side in six innings. He almost bettered Englishman CB Fry's record with Sussex at the turn of the century for the number of first-class hundreds in a row. It was the first time I had heard the name of cricket's ultimate eccentric and snob, Charles Burgess Fry. Fry was long gone but a former opponent and team mate Percy Fender was not. He was one of the oldest players attending the Centenary Test celebrations; then in his 80s, wheelchair-bound and almost completely blind, he was accompanied by a grandson who looked like he could have graduated from Harry Potter's school of magic. Sir Donald Bradman gave the keynote speech at the dinner to commemorate the event, but diplomatically didn't mention Fender's rash predictions, that the boy from

Bowral would be a failure on his first tour of England. The celebration came and went in a blur of Hookes's five fours, Dennis Lillee's masterful bowling, Derek Randall's heroic innings and an identical result from 100 years before. You couldn't have written a better script, although behind the scenes players were being recruited for cricket's greatest revolution, Kerry Packer's World Series Cricket.

It was in this climate that Hughes was selected to tour England. Having not signed up with WSC, Hughes was now seen as wedded to the establishment. The pattern of disunity in the Australian team was set and continued for close to a decade. In the earlier stages of the tour Hughes was overlooked in favour of his Western Australian team mate, Craig Serjeant, who justified his selection by scoring 81 at Lord's on debut. Hughes got his chance in the final Test at the Oval. The night in Australia when Hughes made his Test debut I was probably more nervous than he was. He scored only one run in 53 minutes, which were among the most agonizing of my young life. I spent most of his innings pacing around the living room in my pyjamas while Dad sat in the background trying to watch the cricket. Hookes, who had shown signs of vulnerability outside his off stump, finally justified his selection by charging to a then career best score of 85.

For Australia the tour was a disaster and any chance it had of recovering from a poor start was shattered when the announcement of World Series Cricket was revealed on May 9. Most of the Australian team had signed. It was reported that Hughes was one of the few who had not been asked to join. He later told me that Dennis Lillee, on behalf of Packer, had arranged a meeting with him in a Perth bar to make an offer.

For cricket fans, the summer of 1977-78 was a feast. There was the official Australian team captained by 41-year-old Bobby Simpson against a close to full strength Indian side, while Packer's troupe of the best players in the world played in empty stadiums across the country.

I watched Hughes, wearing his baggy green cap and white sweat bands, struggle, lacking the experience to cope with the wiles of the Indian touring side. He was often criticised for poor stroke selection and looked out of his depth, apart from fleeting moments. I thought he was destined to go the way of the prolific Queensland and briefly Australian player, David Ogilvie, who batted like a statue in the international arena. By the end of the season Hughes had shown little more than most of the other batsmen who made up what was in effect Australia's third team. After another failure in the opening Ashes Test of 1978-79, his future in the game at the top looked bleak. But then Hughes batted for almost eight hours against England to score 129 and recover his Test career (until then he scored only 65 runs in three Test matches). Australia lost the match by seven wickets but Hughes's career was saved.

By the end of the extended season, which also featured three Tests against Pakistan, and because of injury to Australian captain Graham Yallop, my former primary school cricket coach had the top job in Australian sport. Faced with limited options, the Australian selectors chose Hughes to captain Australia against Pakistan in the last Test of the summer. In so doing, Hughes became his state's first Test captain. In a pattern that was rarely repeated under Hughes's stewardship, he recorded the first of his four wins from 28 matches as captain.

Hughes's elevation to captaincy had been remarkable and largely undeserved, a fact noted by his former WA team mates preparing for a truce between Packer and the Australian Cricket Board and their known return to Test cricket. Despite Hughes's motivational speeches to the players he was off the field for much of the game because of an injury. This allowed another newcomer, Andrew Hilditch, to control the on-field play. With a win under his belt, Hughes retained the captaincy and recorded his most successful tour figures for Australia in India in September of 1979. Playing against a top-class spin attack he returned home having scored almost 600 runs in the six Test series and averaging 59. I followed Hughes's scores in brief reports in *The Australian* newspaper. Typical of the era, there was no radio coverage of the tour.

At home the big news was footy finals and the confirmation of the reconciliation between Kerry Packer and the cricket establishment. For fans it meant we would have our best team back playing for Australia. Under Packer, cricket had transformed from merely a sporting contest to a form of entertainment in itself. After a slow start, the multi-camera views of the Nine network and jingoistic marketing made sure the game had maximum exposure. One-day cricket and coloured cricket uniforms ruled by day and night as colour television became a standard household item.

The new dawning found a fresh approach to the international season. The summer of 1979-80 was the first time since the 1912 failed triangular tournament in England that three teams – Australia, West Indies and England – shared a series. Greg Chappell resumed the captaincy and only three players from the Australian team to tour India were selected for the first Test against the West Indies. Packer's Australians were even more galvanised and professionalised from the experience of World Series Cricket. Despite his success in India and his appointment as vice-captain, Hughes still had to prove himself in the full-strength Australian line-up. He duly did, scoring 130 not out in 370 minutes, including keeping the West Indian quartet of Andy Roberts, Michael Holding, Colin Croft and Joel Garner at bay for 244 balls.

The next winter, when Australia toured England for its centenary of Test cricket, Hughes stamped his mark on international cricket with an impressive double at Lord's. While the match was mired in controversy because of delays, Hughes's batting set the home of cricket alight. When long-time English commentator John Arlott was signing off from duties, Hughes notched up scores of 117 and 84, including five sixes. Two of these drives were among the longest ever struck at Lord's. He had batted on every day of the Test match and if his name had been barely known there from the 1977 tour, Hughes had written his own chapter on one of the biggest stages in the world.

Kim Hughes on his way to 213 v India, Adelaide, 1980-81.

Listening to *Test Match Special* on cold winter nights in bed became all the more sweet. If you closed your eyes you could imagine the commentators enjoying their tea and scones as they described the play and read shipping reports and county scores from around the country. For listeners in Australia, despite the inclement weather, Lord's seemed be bathed in sunshine. I slept blissfully during the Centenary Test, occasionally awakened by the excited commentators as Hughes hit another boundary.

Hughes was part of the A list now and I used to imitate his movements at the crease. When I batted in the school team, I copied his closed stance and the way he tugged at his bat, and practised his defence when he walked to the crease. He wore his collar up and moved lightly on his feet down the wicket when he played spin. Hughes was very orthodox, although there were moments of extreme unorthodoxy when he was under pressure. He would occasionally launch all of his weight onto his front knee when he drove the ball through the covers. Having had Hughes as a coach suddenly provided some status for me in the school yard.

With success comes great expectation, but Hughes began the next domestic season poorly. He managed to salvage his summer with a breathtaking double century against the Indians at Adelaide Oval. He followed up his 213 with an undefeated half century on his 27th birthday and celebrated the birth of his twin sons. It marked a celebratory return to the state where he had struggled in district ranks just five years before.

But then there was England 1981. Just mention the words together to a generation of cricket fans and the heartbeat races. With Greg Chappell unavailable, Hughes again captained the Australians abroad. Australia's performance unravelled under the pressure of England's turnaround and the sheer force of performance from Ian Botham and Bob

Willis. After leading the series, Australia eventually lost 3-1 on a tour that became a landmark of poor judgment and misfortune for Australian cricket. This time listening to the *Test Match Special* team proved discomforting as Australia lurched from hope to humiliation.

As the series progressed Australia squandered more opportunities. It seemed that every time I went to bed with Australia in a commanding position, by the time I woke they had lost. Sleep was disturbed on those nights, as the English commentators excitedly described Botham's extraordinary comeback. I may have spent the night tossing and turning but I'm sure sleep for Hughes was harder to come by. The euphoric noise from the English grounds was matched 24 years later with England's unlikely triumph in 2005. Hughes's '81 Australians have a lot to answer for. When I travelled to England three years later to play league cricket in Surrey, the memory still burned strong. My first meal was in front of a video of 'Botham's Ashes' that replayed England's amazing turnaround. It was also repeated the night before I departed for home shores. Australian cricketing friends have similar stories to tell.

When the Australian team returned home, Hughes wasn't the only one who had to face the calamitous failure of his side. I also had to face my friends at school, who never failed to remind me of my association with Hughes. The sounds of discontent in the Australian camp were being heard loud and clear. There was also increasing resentment from his senior team mates Marsh and Lillee, who found Hughes's appointment as Western Australian captain unjust. They of course all had far greater experience and were more accomplished cricketers. The move by WACA authorities effectively ended leadership aspirations for both. Lillee responded to his frustrations by bowling a series of bouncers in the nets at Hughes, sometimes on the morning of a match.

The selectors, by rewarding Hughes for his loyalty to the establishment during the World Series Cricket split, had turned some of his team mates against him. Premature elevation to state and national leadership was as much to blame as anything for the disunity. At the time, Hughes was driven by ambition, unable to weigh up what was best for him and the team. He later admitted that his lack of maturity affected his judgment. Like many at the time, I was unaware of the political power plays within the team that later contributed to Hughes inglorious exit from Test cricket.

Troubled times they may have been but Hughes played what some historians have considered one of the best innings in Test history during this period. Hughes's Boxing Day Test in1981-82 will spark as many memories as Doug Walters spectacular ton from seven years earlier. Hughes batted on an uneven MCG wicket, the same one Bill Lawry said was so bad he wouldn't drive his car on it, arriving at the wicket with Australia precariously placed at 4-26. Wearing his Australian helmet peaked upwards so that his black chin strap was clearly visible, he looked stunned for the first few minutes of the innings. To calm his nerves he frantically opened and closed his eyes and yawned when he stood at the non-striker's end. It was as if he had been interrupted from a long sleep. The shiny red ball really fizzed around the Australian batsmen like one of those backyard tennis balls that had one side heavily soaked in water. The top order batsman looked inept, almost as if they needed to recalibrate their vision.

I wasn't at the MCG to see Hughes play the innings of his life. I was skiing with friends on a calm River Murray on a cloudless day. It was one of those days where the water had a smooth gleam, as if it had been polished. In between skis we listened to Dennis Cometti and the other ABC commentators describe the action. It was Cometti before he started using rehearsed catch phrases. His voice and the constant purring of ski boats intertwined to create the soundtrack of our holiday. When Hughes approached his hundred, we made our way to the front bar of the Mannum pub. We were soon rejoicing in Hughes's unlikely century, and saw the West Indies teetering at 4-10 at stumps. When Viv Richards played on to the last ball of the day we all erupted. It had been the perfect day.

Success for Hughes continued the next summer. As vice-captain he scored 464 runs at an average of 67 as Australia, led by Greg Chappell, atoned for the disaster of '81. Again we sat by the River Murray listening to the drama of the Boxing Day Test. The memories weren't so sweet this time as Alan Border and Jeff Thomson failed by three runs to snatch an unexpected victory.

Australia headed to England for the 1983 World Cup. Greg Chappell again stepped down from the captaincy. Australia stumbled, defeated by Zimbabwe, and left the championship as underperformers. Hughes's ability to captain the side was again questioned. His already strained relationship with some players worsened when he left England before his team mates. This was the beginning of the end, although Hughes then led Australia to a series win against Pakistan, scoring his final Test century and showing class against the wily leg-spinner Abdul Qadir. Qadir was a mix of manic movements and fluency as he drifted to the crease, bouncing and jumping his way to produce a variety of challenging deliveries with more accuracy than any other wrist spinner in the 1980s.

Greg Chappell's final series was unencumbered by the captaincy. His last Test innings saw him bookend his career with three figure scores. Finishing with 182, Chappell broke Bradman's record for total number of Test runs scored. As Chappell neared the milestone, Hughes urged on the man whom he had watched as a teenager score a hundred in his debut Test thirteen years earlier. The way Hughes enthusiastically encouraged his former captain seemed out of place and perhaps showed his longing to be fully accepted.

Chappell's departure provided a stark contrast to the way Hughes's own international career ended just one season later. The home series marked a changing of the guard, ending the careers of not only Chappell but also Marsh and Lillee. With back-to-back Test series against the West Indies scheduled, the famous combination left the game at the right time. It was soon obvious Australia and Hughes were in for a torrid time over the next twelve months. Marsh, who later admitted he would have played on if he had been made captain, was probably the biggest loss. As captain, Marsh would have had the respect of the Australian side and been better equipped to handle the onslaught that followed.

Former Australian captain Graham Yallop titled his account of the 1978-79 Ashes whitewash *Lambs to the Slaughter*. It may have been a more apt description for Hughes's 1984-85 Australians as they faced the best team in the world abroad and at home in back-to-back series, amid a climate of loss of senior players, team disunity and the promise of some lucrative dollars on rebel tours of South Africa. Hughes was under pressure from within and outside his playing circle. The West Indies made a habit out of targeting the opposition captain and they did it with increasing success as the two series wore on.

The warning signs were there when Hughes made a pointless on-field protest against Trinidad and Tobago on the West Indies tour. Team mate and friend Alan Border made an insightful admission in the ABC documentary *Cricket in the '80s* that he doubted Hughes's ability at handling the pressure of the tour when he found his captain sitting in a dazed state in front of his hotel television after getting his hair dreadlocked.

When the contest continued in Australia, it was simply a matter of time until Hughes tendered his emotional resignation from the captaincy after another humiliating loss in the second Gabba Test of the series. The ignominy of a pair at the scene of his greatest triumph, the MCG, signified the end of his Test career after a double failure in Adelaide. As Hughes was facing his final delivery in Test cricket, I was listening to the car radio and rushed inside to see him shuffle across the crease to a Joel Garner yorker. Hughes cast a lonely figure walking off the field, recording his third duck in four innings.

Dropped from the Test side, Hughes was brought back for the Australian one-day side and played in the first day-nighter under lights at the MCG in front of more than eighty thousand people. He failed, run out for nought. He looked like a rabbit caught in a spotlight. This innings sparked the only cricket conversation I had with my brother John, who'd been a commercial pilot for thirty years and shown little interest in sport. 'They should have carried him, like they did that other bloke,' my brother said. The 'other bloke' was Greg Chappell and John was referring to the horror run of ducks against the West Indies and India in the early 1980s. It's funny what sticks in the mind of the non-cricket fan. The days of the Australian selectors rewarding Hughes for his loyalty during World Series Cricket were over. He wasn't picked for the 1985 England tour and never played for Australia again.

Hughes eventually accepted an offer to captain a rebel team to South Africa, but only after discovering Australia had selected players from those already originally signed up with the 'rebels'. It was a bitter blow for Hughes, who had always been loyal to the establishment. Hughes's departure from the national spotlight was rapid. He became a cricketing outcast. After playing in two poorly publicised (in Australia) tours of South Africa, Hughes returned to contest an acrimonious court case with the WA Cricket Association. He won the case and again played for Western Australia. But by the late 1980s it was obvious he wasn't the player he had been and he soon bowed out of the game. It was a subdued ending. There was no fond farewell, just a failed closure to his international career. As I remember he was run out in his last first-class innings at Adelaide Oval, after struggling at the crease barely into double figures. It was a less than impressive performance. He had come full circle from when I had watched him bat in the district final just before his meteoric rise.

By this time I was in my mid-twenties and had moved beyond the hero worship of teenage years. Yet I still felt a sense of anger at the way Hughes's career ended and the lack of acknowledgement from modern day cricket fans. The anger remained and eventually I wrote about Hughes's career. I wrote to him while I was researching, but he never responded. I showed the article to a friend who said he hadn't realised Hughes had played with so much success. He just remembered the tears.

Two years later I met Hughes at a restaurant at Yalingup in the south-west of Western Australia where I was holidaying. I didn't recognise him at first. He was then in his mid-forties and looked overweight, although there was something about his swagger that was the giveaway. Later in the night I introduced myself and we arranged to meet in Perth. When we did, he looked to still be carrying the disappointment of how his Australian career had ended. He told me how he had mended fences with old foes and it was a time of optimism. Hughes was again being welcomed back into the fold by the Western Australian Cricket association.

It seemed we had all moved on.

Chapter 15

The Mystery Man of Australian Cricket: Jack Moroney

Life as a teenager can be strange. More often than not you are consumed by what others think of you. But when you occasionally stop to look beyond your own life, matters of social conscience arise. For some reason, in my teen years I became fixated with capital punishment. The year of the dawning was 1977 when the death penalty was reintroduced in the United States. That was when I first read about John Spenkelink, who was on death row and eventually executed for murdering a hitchhiker he picked up in the mid-west of America.

'Them without the capital get the punishment,' is what Spenkelink is alleged to have said before they turned sparky on. He was the second to go down death row after Gary Gilmore almost ran to the firing squad three years earlier. While Gilmore's namesake was opening the bowling for Australia, the convicted felon made international headlines when he requested and received the death penalty for murdering two people in Utah. Through the Gilmour name my joint worlds of cricket and obsession with the death penalty collided.

It was the idea of an act I thought was unjust that made me focus on the death penalty in the United States. This was also when I recognised another, albeit far less significant, injustice. This injustice revolved around the Test career of former Australian opener Jack Moroney. He was an Australian cricketer from the late 1940s and early 1950s, described by cricket writer David Frith as the 'mystery man of Australian cricket'.

I first noticed Moroney in *The Courage Australian Book of Test Cricket 1877-1974*, a compilation of scorecards and summaries from Australian Test matches. Scanning through the decades, I read about the 1950-51 Ashes series that documented Moroney's only Ashes Test appearance, resulting in a pair of ducks. But there was something about this double failure and his subsequent dropping from the team that seemed unjust. Over time I wondered who this Australian opener was and why his time in the spotlight was so fleeting. Pictures of the match are scarce, although I found photos of Moroney that reveal a friendly appearance, a bit like a farmer greeting you at his front gate with a warm smile and firm handshake.

When I read about Moroney's humiliation it was during the lead-up to the Centenary Test staged in Melbourne in March 1977. The one-off match marked the anniversary of the official start of Test cricket and all living Ashes participants were invited to Melbourne for a week-long celebration. It must have been hard for Moroney to join a celebration of a contest in which he had been a complete failure. He could have been excused for not attending or for greeting Sir Donald Bradman, the key speechmaker at the official dinner, in a slightly cold manner. Bradman, after all, had been one of the selectors when Moroney was ingloriously dumped after the rain-affected Test of 1950-51. The Don had struggled himself on a wet wicket in Brisbane in his debut in 1928-29 (admittedly he too was dropped, but I thought his early experience may have given him some empathy toward Moroney). Australia's most dominant presence was also there when they brought down the guillotine to finish Moroney's Test career after he played once more against the West Indies in the summer of 1951-52.

Cricket historian Warwick Franks interviewed Moroney in the 1990s, finding him to be a 'charming raconteur full of ironic self deprecation.' Franks also noted his interviewee to be a 'brilliant batsman'. Yet along the way this appreciation of Moroney's talents appear to have been lost in the wider cricketing community.

In the late 1990s I heard Moroney interviewed by ABC radio's Jim Maxwell during the lunch break of an Australian Test against South Africa. He sounded friendly and gentle. Maxwell diplomatically focused on Moroney's achievements against South Africa, where he once scored a century in each innings of a Test match, and avoided the Ashes Test of 1950-51. But that was what I most wanted to hear about. What must it have been like for Moroney to be defined by one major failure after decades of playing a sport? Moroney averaged more than fifty in 57 first class matches, as well as scoring two centuries in a single Test against South Africa, so he could play. So what was the path Moroney trod before and after Brisbane, 1950-51?

He was born in Macksville on the mid-north coast of New South Wales in 1917 when his father was teaching at Eungai. Moroney went to school locally before attending St Joseph's College in Sydney in his final year. He stood out among his peers, with the sports master Brother Henry describing Moroney as 'the most talented boy [he] had coached, even ahead of Stan McCabe.' He was a late starter in district ranks because of teacher training and an early appointment in the Casino District. Work in the army and RAAF further delayed his entry into grade cricket until he was 26. Two years later Moroney made his debut for NSW against Queensland in the match to mark first class cricket's official return after the Second World War. His progress for his state was slow, a bit like the way he batted in his early days at first class level. By season's end he'd played just three matches, averaging 27. A year passed before he represented NSW again, but when he did he scored 96 against the visiting Indians for a full strength NSW team featuring Australian players Morris, Miller, Lindwall and Toshack. Moroney's 96 took just over two hours and he dominated a second wicket stand of 153 with Morris. He finished the 1947-48 season in an even more confident manner, making 533 runs with an average of 44.

The next summer saw Moroney cement his place in the NSW team, with his first domestic hundred (122) against Queensland. Scores of 98 against South Australia and an undefeated hundred facing the Victorian attack brought him to the notice of Australia's selectors. A double century (217) in the Kippax-Oldfield testimonial and Test trial in February 1949 confirmed his talent, with Moroney scoring his second hundred in just 79 minutes. When it came to the time for Australia to select its side to tour South Africa, Moroney's average of 81 had him placed second on the national list, bettered only by his state team mate and Australian opening batsman, Arthur Morris.

The Australian tour of South Africa later that year had controversy at its core. First, Sid Barnes refused to tour because of claims of poor pay, and later the world's best all-rounder Keith Miller was excluded from the Australian side because of modest form in the domestic competition. However, there was strong circumstantial evidence Miller was paying for his differences with Bradman in 1948. Miller was eventually included when Bill Johnston was injured in a car crash, but Barnes's stance against the authorities stayed and opened the door for Moroney. Then aged 32, it is said he understated his age by three years to improve his chances. Perhaps it did, and in his only tour as an Australian batsman he prospered under the relatively laid-back approach of the whimsical skipper Lindsay Hassett.

Wearing the Australian colours comfortably, Moroney scored three first class hundreds before being run out for a duck in his only innings in the first Test at Johannesburg. A Test score of 87 at Cape Town preceded his century in each innings of the fourth Test at Ellis Park. Moroney made history with 118 and an undefeated 101 in a match celebrated by 20-year-old Neil Harvey's completion of a trio of centuries in successive Tests (he scored a hundred in the next one as well). Notwithstanding his increasing success, RS Whitington acerbically described Moroney's batting in the second innings as resembling a 'purposeless porpoise'. By the tour's end, Australia had won the series 4-0, with Moroney completing the trip with 352 Test runs at 50. His international future, at least in the short term, appeared bright.

The 1950-51 Ashes series was the first chapter of life without Bradman, the first Ashes series since 1926 without his on-field presence. England had proved disappointing on its previous tour four years earlier. Led by a well-past-his-best Wally Hammond, they had lost 3-0. Demoralisation at the hands of Bradman's Invincibles at home followed in 1948, as did an historic 3-1 loss against the West Indies. Subsequently England entered the Ashes series as underdogs. In the lead-up to the Tests, Moroney's confidence was riding high. A score of 113 in New South Wales's opening fixture against Queensland and a half-century against the visiting English side boded well for an anticipated Ashes debut in the first Test in Brisbane.

To say the cricketing gods were unkind to Moroney is something of an understatement. Out for a duck in the first over caught at leg gully, Australia's newest opening batsman attracted the wrath of leading cricket scribe Neville Cardus. The music critic cum cricket writer described Moroney's dismissal as 'careless… without intellectual comment'. It was a display of English superiority from a writer considered by many as a snob despite his working class Manchester origins. Cardus, often known more for romanticised prose than accurate reporting, should have realised that Moroney had fallen for the same trap as Bradman during the 1948 tour of England.

Australia struggled at the crease, scoring its lowest total at home for thirteen years and eventually making it to 228, courtesy of Harvey's contribution of 74. Heavy overnight rain and an absence of the modern use of covers saw England, batting on a sticky wicket, slumping to 7-68 before captain Bill Brown shrewdly declared. When Australia lost its first three wickets without a run on the board, including Moroney, the English captain's decision of an early closure seemed vindicated. Despite the seriousness of Australia's predicament and giving an insight into the nature of the Australian captain, Hassett announced, 'Well, I suppose some poor bastard's gotta start this innings.'

For Moroney his Ashes debut had gone from bad to worse. By lunch on the second day he was back in the pavilion with a pair of ducks next to his name. In the second innings he was given out LBW after padding up to Trevor Bailey. The umpire's decision seemed a dubious one but nonetheless consigned Moroney to an unenviable place in cricket history. By tea, Australia had also declared early at 7-32, with Harvey again top-scoring, this time with just 12 runs. With the pitch still playing up and England needing

193 to win the match the visitors limped to 6-30 by stumps. Day two had been so eventful that retired Australian batsman and cricket journalist Jack Fingleton later described the events as being 'the craziest and maddest Test of all time.' Predictably the match was over by the third and final day, when England were bowled out for 122. Len Hutton's resourceful undefeated 62 helped the visitors recover from 8-46 but in the end it was not enough.

After such a promising lead in, Moroney's international summer was over after just five balls. His replacement, Ken Archer, was a younger, more graceful player who was athletic in the field. It seemed the selectors were sending a message to any Australian aspirants and youth was at the heart of it. It would have been easy for him to lose faith but Moroney simply returned to domestic cricket and continued churning out the runs, scoring 413 runs at 41 that season.

The next season proved to be Moroney's swansong, although a final opportunity at Test level followed when he was picked for the fourth Test of the summer against the West Indies. Moroney's final Test was remembered for Australia's unlikely one wicket win when Bill Johnston and Doug Ring put on 38 for the final wicket. Moroney's contribution of 26 and 5 were not enough for a batsman entering his mid-thirties to retain his position. Moroney's final first class match coincided with the debut of a 16-year-old Ian Craig against South Australia, providing a reflection of where Australia's cricket selectors were heading. Moroney's score of 38 took his season tally for New South Wales to 588 runs at 58, helping his side to that season's Sheffield Shield.

In the end, Moroney's Test career was short but eventful. Averaging 34 from his seven tests, he scored more than 4000 first class runs at an average of 52. Continuing with first grade cricket in Newcastle until the age of 48 Moroney averaged more than 50 over three seasons. From what Moroney later said, his love for the game remained, as did fond memories of life as a first class and Test cricketer.

Despite the words, in the back of my mind I still wonder how often he thought back to that rain drenched day at the Gabba all those years before and wished things had turned out differently.

Chapter 16

Hookesy Why?

The word 'Hookesy', taken out of context of time and place, sounds as if you are describing something fun and playful, perhaps with a touch of mystery. Maybe that's one way of summing up the cricketing career and life of former Australian Test cricketer David Hookes. He was someone who arrived in our consciousness in a blaze of glory during his golden summer of 1977 and departed so tragically, before anyone had the chance to say goodbye, at the age of 48 after an altercation at a hotel.

Hookes had a sense of adventure and confidence reserved normally for fictional sporting heroes. All the girls at school loved him and the boys envied him. It was only later in life we discovered that, like all humans, he had foibles.

Hookes's name ultimately became a symbol of unfulfilled potential yet in some ways it is misleading. At first class level in Australia, long considered the strongest domestic competition in the world, Hookes performed consistently over three decades. So well in fact that he finished his career as the competition's leading run scorer, notching up 178 first class games, registering 32 hundreds at a healthy average of 43. But it was consistent success at Test level that was lacking.

Hookes's Test record extended to just 23 matches over eight years, which surprised many, but apparently not Hookes. Always one to speak his mind, he acknowledged a lack of intense hunger to succeed at the top level and spoke freely about his inability to play top-class spin bowling.

After Hookes's spectacular entry into international cricket, it was always going to be difficult to live up to expectations. He wasn't called 'the next Bradman', but the predictions weren't far off. Not that he appeared too concerned about what others thought. That was one of the reasons why he was so popular among cricket fans. His general irreverence was reinforced by playing under Ian Chappell and made him appear slightly rebellious.

And Hookes proved he wasn't simply bluffing. In his debut season he was part of a South Australian team that went on strike when Ian Chappell objected to the selectors' lack of consultation with the captain for an eastern states tour. Chappell eventually backed down and the tour proceeded, with SA going on to win the Sheffield Shield that season. But the incident had grabbed front page headlines and the moment, although not obvious then, gave an insight into the way player power was heading.

Hookes's batting in his debut season of first class cricket wasn't spectacular, although he made an impression because of the attacking and flamboyant way in which he played. Managing 395 runs at 32, Hookes failed to score a century. My main memory of him that summer was of his blasting a quick-fire 40 in a one-day game at the Gabba in Brisbane. I was in Queensland as part of an interstate tour for the South Australian primary school team, who watched the game. I remember the small crowd of around five thousand people making the loudest noise I had heard outside of a football crowd at home. South Australia lost but Hookes's cameo made the day worthwhile and showed why he was such a favourite with young cricket fans.

I had a connection of sorts with Hookes. His father worked in a business owned by the family of my friends, the twins Gary and Greg. I heard about Hookes's first overseas cricketing stint in England, where he played league cricket with Dulwich in 1975, creating notoriety in one match when he hit every ball of a six ball over for six.

The twins who were also sporting-minded shared my passion for cricket, and they regularly updated me about Hookes's progress, which heightened as he went on his record run-scoring spree in the lead up to the Centenary Test.

A sporting rivalry developed between the twins and me. They knew I was a fan of Kim Hughes, who hadn't then played for Australia. The competition intensified when Hookes was selected to play for Australia in the Centenary Test . I saw Hookes interviewed on television after he'd peeled off five hundreds in six first class innings in March of 1977. He scored 163, 9, 185, 101, 135 and 156 – making Hookes only the second player in the history of first class cricket to register centuries in each innings of successive games. It was the first time I had heard the phrase 'purple patch' used by Hookes when he spoke modestly about his selection. It was as if we were listening to a bloke down at the pub, talking about what he was planning for the weekend.

Hookes had really come from obscurity that season to earn a place in the Australian side. Having foregone South Australia's tour of the eastern states because of year-twelve exams, there was even talk about him returning to club cricket. That changed when his score of 163 out of a total of 290 against Victoria placed him on a trajectory to Australian selection. Not that all were convinced, since Australia's front-line bowlers were away on a tour of New Zealand.

There was a photo in the local paper of Hookes on one knee, sweeping the ball over the mid-wicket fence, and another of him driving the ball through the covers. His stance was unconventional, because his legs were crossed and he seemed to be off balance. The ball is visible speeding away to the boundary, giving some indication of the power of the stroke. Hookes was using his old bandaged bat, which looked out of place.

Hookes blasts his way into the Centenary Test, March 1977.

It had been a dramatic and unexpected rise for Hookes, whose first outing for South Australia had been just two years before. On debut he had scored 55 against the West

Indies, with a panache and sense of confidence that teenagers can possess. And here he was about to play on one of the largest sporting stages in the world. In the week leading up to the Centenary Test, a writer for *Boys Own Annual* would have been hard pressed to come up with a more colourful story. Yet here it was. 'Young, good-looking batsman gets selected to make his debut in the biggest match of all time.' In his autobiography, Hookes wrote that he had to be shown by Gary Gilmour how to operate the shower in his bathroom at the Melbourne Hilton Hotel. He also naively believed his team mate when he told him to make sure he didn't step on the tramlines across Wellington Parade, to avoid being electrocuted.

The Centenary Test was one of the most anticipated matches in the game's history. Australia Post issued six stamps celebrating the first ever Test in 1877 and a specially minted gold coin designed for the toss.

All the surviving players from Ashes contests were invited to attend the week long celebration. The first ever cricketing crowd of one hundred thousand was expected to show up for the first day. (They didn't – the attendance is listed as 61,316.)

Even Greg Chappell showed signs of nerves when he struggled for almost four hours for an unconvincing 40 without a single boundary in Australia's first innings of 138. Hookes managed 17 but could easily have been out LBW first ball if Bob Willis hadn't overstepped the mark. Hookes showed some of the style that had seen him selected, with two searing cover drives before following a Chris Old delivery that bounced more than he expected into Tony Greig's safe hands at slip.

England batted just as poorly as Australia, managing only 90 and so it was game on. Hookes's first innings was merely the entrée to a boundary-filled second innings score of 56. His post lunch mauling of English captain Tony Greig, striking five boundaries in a row, defines his cricketing career. When he was out soon after, again caught by Greig, Hookes signed off with a verbal volley. Little did we know how this signature would also bookend his life.

Australia won the game by 45 runs, the same result in the first Test, 100 years before, but it was Hookes who was the hero across the country. His batting even drew comparisons with left-handed greats Frank Woolley, Neil Harvey and Graeme Pollock.

When Australia won the game Hookes walked off the field triumphantly with his team mates. I imagined that he would have revelled in the post-match celebrations but later read he felt so out of place that he quietly caught an early plane from Melbourne back to Adelaide to spend a quiet night with family and friends.

Hookes on debut had scaled dizzying heights and become the target of the recruiters of World Series Cricket. He was the poster boy of the breakaway competition and played well enough to score a Super Test hundred. Financially lucrative it may have been but in many ways the move stalled his development as a batsman.

What could have happened to Hookes's career had he not played in that match is interesting to speculate. It is likely he would have toured England, but with a less prominent role. He would certainly have been in the front runners to play in the establishment side that played India that summer. If he'd done this he would have gained valuable experience against top-class spinners, at home and then later on the sub-con-tinent when Australia toured there in 1979. Perhaps most importantly Hookes would have avoided a debilitating injury he suffered when his jaw was broken from an Andy Roberts bouncer. His time out of the game stretched for several months, including a six-week period where his diet consisted of liquidised food eaten via a straw. The mental scars of the injury lingered until Hookes used hypnotherapy to get over it.

But his cricketing path was set with WSC, in which he played a major role. The sight of a breathless Hookes performing push-ups, and then wearing a motorbike helmet and hitting Andy Roberts for a six, coinciding with the 'C'mon Aussie C'mon' was part of the television promotion that was continually played. Hookes contributed significant innings, including 116 in a Super Test against the West Indies at Waverly. He finished with 770 runs at 38 in the Super Tests, which was an impressive figure considering he was playing against the best fast bowlers in the world.

Timing and form didn't coincide for Hookes for extended periods at the top level. Injury had a habit of hampering him at critical points of his career. One was just after the reconciliation between the cricket establishment and WSC. He scored 43 and 37 against the West Indies in the first Test of a twin series involving England, but tore his hamstring and was out of action for the remainder of the international summer. Picked to tour Pakistan in February of 1980, Hookes's weakness against spin was exposed and he played in just one Test, scoring a pair and making just 10 runs from the limited opportunities on the three Test tour. It must have been a shattering experience for the player who was the focus of such attention just a few years before.

Hookes's career continued on its downward slide the next summer. The decline was so marked by December of 1980 that he was dropped from the South Australian team, before the selectors led by Barry Jarman – in a move of great foresight – picked him as an all-rounder later that season. His ascendancy during the next two years almost matched his previous decline. With his confidence renewed and the responsibility of captain, Hookes scored 700 runs and led his state to a Sheffield Shield win.

My connection with Hookes continued, but not as I would have liked. He bowled me out for a duck with his left-arm medium pacers in a district match against West Torrens. Despite his obvious lack of pace off the wicket, Hookes's delivery broke the stump. The embarrassment of being dismissed second ball was heightened when the fielder ran up to me to ask where they could get another stump. Former Australian opening batsman Rick Darling also played for West Torrens that day and patrolled the covers so efficiently he made the area in front of square on the off side seem much smaller than it was.

The summer of 1982-83 revealed as much about Hookes's ability as it did about his limitations. He had scored 622 runs for SA in four matches before he got the call-up to play his first Test since his failure in Pakistan. Part of Hookes's flying start to the season was his century in each innings (137 and 107) against Victoria at the Adelaide Oval. At the time his second ton of the match was the fastest authentic hundred made by an Australian. It took 43 minutes and 34 balls. Like a schoolyard bully, Hookes treated Victoria's pace bowlers Peter King, Rod McCurdy and Shaun Graf as if they were primary school cricketers playing in the first eleven.

The day Hookes scored his record-breaking hundred I was coaching at the South Australian Cricket Association's indoor nets. I knew that Victoria had given the home side 30 overs to score 272, and so didn't bother paying much notice. That was until I heard the clunking sound of the ball hitting the boundary. The noise sounded like someone pelting rocks on a roof as Hookes's powered his way to a second hundred of the match with 17 fours, most of which rebounded noisily off the metallic signs attached to the picket fence. Not satisfied with simply pounding the boundaries, he also cleared the fence three times. Sadly I didn't get to see any of the innings, but I can say at least I heard some of it!

Yet as much as the summer showed how far Hookes had advanced, it also revealed his inability to convert starts to three figures. His 344 runs at 49 included three fifties and a top score of 68 as Australia won that Ashes series 2-1. By the end of the summer Hookes, as Australia's vice-captain, notched up his only Test hundred against Sri Lanka. His 143 not out included a century in the session between lunch and tea.

From there it was downhill, despite captaining Australia against India in the 1983 World Cup. Not for the first time, Hookes's remarks that Kim Hughes was not the number one choice as captain led to a dressing down from the Australian Cricket Board. Modest performances for Australia on the 1984 tour of the West Indies were partly attributable to a knee injury that had plagued Hookes during the domestic season

Hookes's Test career was over by the time he was 30 when he was briefly recalled to the Australian team against New Zealand and India in the summer of 1985-86. His final innings was a first ball duck, perhaps fittingly, against a spin bowler. By the mid-1980s the Australian team was moving toward a new phase and players from Hookes's era (apart from Border) were seen as part of the past. This was confirmed five days after he was dropped, when he scored 243 against New South Wales off just 254 deliveries (including ten sixes and twenty-six fours) yet failed to be included in the touring team to New Zealand.

A triple century (306) against Tasmania the following season helped Hookes create an Australian record for a partnership with Wayne Phillips. Despite being stripped of the captaincy, he continued to play for South Australia, finishing at the end of 1991-92 as the leading runs-scorer in the history of the Sheffield Shield.

Although I played against Hookes at district level I never played under him. In what I heard and saw of him on the field I didn't think he had the qualities of a captain. Hookes didn't appear to have the empathy to deal with the range of personalities that make a team. Yet oddly enough for a player who had spent much of his career without a close mentor, he showed signs of being an influential Victorian coach. (As a player, he developed an intense rivalry with that state, and almost transferred to it in the late 1980s.) His ability to think laterally also added to his coaching stocks. He once ran out Dean Jones from first slip after noticing how far Victoria's best batsmen batted outside of his crease.

Just before he became the Victorian coach I interviewed him for a community radio station in Adelaide, where he politely knocked back any suggestion that his work in the media would give him a conflict of interest. He provided a balanced view and gave the impression that at least in some ways he had matured.

The last time I heard his voice was on the radio. He was talking enthusiastically about Victoria's amazing performance just after his team had successfully chased New South Wales's total of 445. You could hear the euphoria in his voice. Hookes had a good relationship with young cricketers and one could sense that he enjoyed the win as much as the players did. Perhaps with the advantage of experience, he knew when to savour a moment.

It was a strange feeling on that Monday morning in late January, 2004, waking to the news that Hookes was in a critical condition in hospital after a fight at a hotel the night before. As the day progressed, the news became more dire and when I heard the words 'brain dead' the truth hit home. Dad rang with the news that Hookes had died. 'He's gone.' And with those words there was a feeling of loss for Hookes and his family and many friends, but also for part of my childhood that had vanished.

At the time of his tragic death, Hookes looked certain

to make a large impression as the coach of the Victorian team that within a few months would win the Sheffield Shield for the first time in more than a decade. It was a shocking and senseless death, although the media coverage was as outrageous as it was bias. The lack of accuracy about Hookes's private life and treatment of the man as if he were a deity was wrong and told us as much about parts of the media as it did about Hookes. For a bloke who told it like it was in the media, I'm sure he would have seen the irony.

Such was the complexity of Hookes that he was someone we all thought we knew but later realised we didn't know at all.

Chapter 17

Death and Cricket

Finality and themes of death have long been connected with cricket. The one chance rule tends to exist more in cricket than in other sports; in general, if you are a batsman, you don't get a second chance. The exception is rare, such as when Greg Chappell was bowled out during an interstate match in the 1960s but later called back. On that occasion a swallow had flown across the pitch colliding with the ball and killing the bird mid-flight. The ball having been diverted went on to hit Chappell's wicket. The unfortunate swallow then took pride of place in a glass container at the Adelaide Oval museum.

The notion of death is central to the language of cricket. There are victims, batsmen perish, and they are entombed in pairs. The game has been described as a pitched battle. Bowlers dispatch batsmen and knock them over. Batsmen, it is said at times, defend as if their life depended on it. When a bowler completes his six deliveries it is over.

Despite perceptions of a glamorous existence, life as a professional cricketer can be fraught. As revealed by Peter Roebuck in his fascinating analysis of the life of a county cricketer, *It Never Rains: a cricketer's lot*, the game often attracts serious minds and sensitive characters. David Frith noted in his book *Silence of the Heart* that proportionately the number of cricketers who take their own life is much higher than in the general population. Obituaries are also an integral part of cricket's bible, the *Wisden Cricketers' Almanack.*

Stories of Australian cricketers dying during war are well known, perhaps none more famous than fast bowler 'Tibby' Cotter, who perished in the First World War (historians continue to debate whether it was at the charge of Beersheba as part of the 4th Lighthorse Brigade, or in a trench). Then there was the young and promising Ross Gregory, who was shot down over Europe in the Second World War. The possibility of wartime death led another pilot, Keith Miller, to define the pressure on a cricket field as 'nothing compared to having a Messerschmitt up your arse'.

Instances of death on a cricket field are rare. Martin Bedkober's death in a Queensland grade game was a warning to all cricketers in the 1970s. The season it happened Thomson and Lillee's brand of pace bowling and aggression was devastating the West Indies' batting line up. The circumstances of Bedkober's death – struck in the chest by a rising delivery – were not lost on the tourists. The Windies went on to dominate world cricket for almost two decades with brilliance and intimidation carried out by a frightening combination of four pace bowlers.

Dad once told me about the death of a different sort on the cricket field. It happened in Adelaide during the 1950s, when a parklands cricketer was shot dead on a picturesque ground on the western edge of the city called Railway's Oval. My father described to me how a policeman talked the gunman down, winning an award for bravery in the process.

Bravery was something that New South Wales cricketer Dr Claude Tozer had shown plenty of in his time serving in the forces during the First World War. He served with distinction at Gallipoli and on the Western front, winning the DSO. Promotion to the rank of Major for his service as a doctor on the French battlefields followed and when he returned to Australia it was with shrapnel in the base of his skull.

And yet when it came to strange deaths associated with cricket few could match his.

The story, set in Australia in the 1920s, reads more like a Hollywood movie script than fact. The headline: Star cricketer and war hero slain by Sydney socialite. The fact that the murderer was Dorothy Mort, his lover and patient, only added to the hysteria. In the trial some weeks after the murder, she was found not guilty on the grounds of insanity. Mort died two decades later in the asylum. The papers were abuzz with the news and the cricketing community shocked and dismayed. How could one of their own finish up the centrepiece of such a controversial story?

Some clues surrounding Tozer's death were recently revealed as part of an exhibition of Sydney crime files from the 1920s. The images appear mundane, almost routine at

Death scene, Dr Claude Tozer, 1920, Sydney.

first glance. The deceased is neatly dressed in a suit and tie, which are hardly ruffled. His head is on a slant, as if Tozer was taking an afternoon nap. The sitting room he is in looks well ordered. The only apparent disturbance is a bloodied white sheet. It remains as evidence, perhaps of an attempt to clean the scene.

Tozer had been killed by fatal gunshot wounds to the head and heart, although in the photo it isn't obvious. It looks as if the murderer approached from behind. He probably had no idea it was coming. It was two hours before the maid, Florence Fizzelle, discovered the body. Mort was later discovered in her bedroom semi-conscious, having taken laudanum, and with a gunshot wound to the chest.

It was the end of what could have been a successful Test career. Tozer's entry into first class cricket was interrupted because of his medical studies and work as a doctor. A debut hundred against Queensland the season after the war followed, while dual half centuries for an Australia side against the MCC in 1920 confirmed his potential Test status. Just before Christmas he was selected as captain for New South Wales against Queensland on New Year's Day. His fatal mistake was deciding to tell his patient and lover that their affair was over and that he was getting married.

On the day he was murdered, Tozer watched Australia dominate the first Ashes Test at Sydney, with state team mate Alan Kippax's father at the SCG. Tozer was from all reports popular with his team mates and viewed with even greater respect by younger members for his war service. Why he decided to become involved with a patient, a move that jeopardised his position as a doctor, is unknown. It prompts speculation about the effect the war had on him, being so close to so much death and destruction.

Tozer is only part of the story. What became of Mr Mort, left to raise two children on his own and dealing with the humiliation of a public scandal that ensued? What was the damage to the children, brought up without their biological mother? Then there is the woman Tozer was to marry; how did she cope in the shadow of this tragedy hanging over her life? Like many actions consuming just moments, there were many implications.

When the news broke, Tozer's former team mates wore black armbands as a mark of respect. Imagine the reaction in the dressing room to the news that a colleague had been murdered. No doubt cricketers had affairs in this era, although they weren't reported on. What was the response from other high profile players who may have been carrying on affairs themselves, and what would the players have known about Tozer's personal situation? Maybe he kept to himself.

Chapter 18

The Stories of Ben Hollioake & Les Favell

When it comes to personal connection with Test cricketers who have died prematurely, I have two. Both very different cricketers and people, Les Favell and Ben Hollioake were two who left the game with much to offer, one as a player, the other as a mentor and coach.

It's hard to believe that it's more than twenty years since Les Favell died. He was the rock of South Australian cricket for close to two decades and his loss created a major gap in the state's cricketing intelligence. The stocky right-hander's distinctive slicked-back hair was almost as trademark as his attacking batting style. His friendly and positive nature was reflected in Favell's calm and controlled leadership. He played Test cricket, although his modest returns limited his appearances to just nineteen. Favell was better known for his run-scoring ability in the Sheffield Shield and captaining South Australia a record 95 times, an era in which he mentored a number of future formative figures in the game.

Favell was a no-nonsense sort of bloke, who played straight when he managed people. He helped mould Ian

Chappell's attacking style of captaincy but without the emphasis on confrontation. He was too old school for that. Favell looked and behaved like an old-fashioned bloke.

Sadly Les died young. He was just 57 when he succumbed to cancer of the kidney. I had met him three years before, as part of a cricket-coaching clinic for *The Advertiser*. It was a brief crossing of paths, but his influence lingers and the memory of two weeks driving around South Australia and teaching primary-school students remains.

It was the summer of 1984 when we started our mini odyssey from the Adelaide Oval car park on our way to the north of the state. Favell was at the wheel of an old Torana. I was sitting in the passenger's seat feeling a little overawed. As the car rolled out onto War Memorial Drive I felt surprised but privileged at being given equal coaching status with a former player of Favell's stature. I wondered why I'd received the call up. I was, after all, a mere district cricketer more often playing B-Grade for Kensington than in the seniors. Perhaps the state team was away on interstate duties.

Favell was dressed in his business pants and white cricket shirt, the type with the stiff collars that players in the 1950s and '60s wore. I was in the more modern shinier tracksuit pants and soft open-collared Gray Nicolls white cricket shirt. It was the look of the experienced and the young.

As someone who was pretty familiar with cricket's history, I was keen to talk to Les about his role in the game. Driving out of the city and onto the Main North Road, and after the initial pleasantries, I thought about what to ask him. Where would I begin? I didn't want to sound too eager for information or that all I wanted to know was about his playing career. He asked me what it was like playing for Kensington, and what I thought of the standard of district cricket. Les even asked if I had a girlfriend and what she made of me being on the cricket field so much. He had a cricket-playing son Alan who was around my age, so perhaps he was trying to sound out the youth view. I thought about the pressures that Alan faced, being the son of Les. I had the impression Les allowed his son to be his own man and would have been happy regardless of what sport Alan played. For a man who must have seen a lot, on and off the field, Les was a gentle character.

Once we reached the outskirts of the city, the conversation gained momentum, like an opening partnership that had taken the shine off the new ball. We were soon talking about opening the batting and the approach to the first few overs. I spoke about the apprehension I felt when going in at the top of the order. In response I got the Favell creed: 'I used to always treat the first ball of an innings the way I would treat any ball when I was set. If it is a half-volley you hit it through the covers for four.'

He was true to his word as well. He'd been out the opening ball in a first class match and also hit the first ball of a match for six.

'But you're not set, how do you play as if you are?' I somewhat hesitantly asked.

'If you were batting in the nets and the first ball was a half-volley, you'd drive it, wouldn't you?

I figured he had a point and that you have to be in a state of mind ready to hit the first ball for four. Not that he forced the issue. Les was a subtle persuader, and that perhaps as much as anything explained why he was such a successful captain. I had the feeling he was working me out as the conversation developed.

I realised how refreshing Favell's approach to the game was. When I played cricket I put so much pressure on myself, I placed a premium on not getting out first and scoring runs second. I was envious of the way Favell approached and played the game. He made cricket seem simple, just as I did but only in rare moments when I was having an on day. I tended to over analyse the game. His joy seemed to be greater. Mine was weighed down by the what-ifs; he had been prepared to take his chances, and it was after all simply a game. To me it seemed to mean more.

It struck me how odd it was that I, as a fringe A grade player, could consider I took the game more seriously than a former Test cricketer. But then maybe not. Les's passion for the game shone through, while mine was acutely calibrated to my success with the bat. At the time I was eager to get back into the Kensington A grade team and remember worrying about the challenge that lay ahead.

When Les spoke I got the sense that there was no over analysis. As a captain he must have made the game seem simple for any complex personalities in his team who tried to make it complicated. The game was a simple affair and to be played aggressively but with a fair sense of play. Favell didn't have much time for those who didn't take the chance to try and win. This attitude was reflected in the way he batted and captained.

Sitting next to him was as close as I would get to such an important part of the game's history. Not so much because of what he personally achieved but more what he was part of. I was interested to find out about his time in the Australian team playing alongside the likes of Richie Benaud, Neil Harvey and Alan Davidson. I also knew he'd played in the Tied Test against the West Indies at the Gabba in 1960-61.

The only images I had in my memory of Favell was of black and white photos and limited newsreel footage of him hitting the winning runs in a Test match at Adelaide Oval. I wondered what the dressing room was like when Lindsay Kline and Ian Meckiff tried to scramble that last run, the moment so well captured in the famous photo, when Jo Solomon threw down the stumps to tie the game. Les spoke amusingly about how commentator Alan McGilvray had caught the early plane home because he thought the match would end in a draw. He also laughed at the large numbers who said they were at the ground on the last day despite the crowd being in the low thousands. I wondered what it was like for Favell to forever be linked with such an important part of the history of the game, a part that could never be taken away from him. If I'd known what lay ahead I would have asked more.

Favell had scored a hundred in a Test match in India, hadn't he? The topic of the subcontinent soon came up. I had previously heard from Barry Jarman about how hard life was touring India and was keen to hear Favell's version of events. Would it match up to the cockroach-infested accounts of subcontinent hotels? It did. Favell had written his name into the history books with a Test hundred in India, but the conversation soon moved on. During the two weeks of our journey, I hunted down Favell's autobiography, *By Hook or By Cut*. There's a picture in it of Favell's baseball-playing days where he represented South Australia. The one that stands out is of him sitting on a bench with team mates. Favell's face is battered and bruised. He looks happy enough, like he's encouraging his team at the national Australian championships in Brisbane.

The book's oddly coloured green cover shows Favell playing his favourite shot, the back foot cut. In the image, he is portrayed from side on, providing a profile of the batsman's nuggetty but well-balanced frame and determined expression. The simplicity of the picture says much about the way Favell played cricket. The book's title also defined the way he batted, with an emphasis on aggression. Batting was fun and about taking it up to the bowlers. When he was at the crease he moved minimally, with no excesses. They all seemed to play that way in the 1950s and '60s, or was it just the way the jumpy black and white footage made it look?

Young female teachers serving their time in the regions invariably met Les and I at the school oval's entrance as an excited group of students waited, sitting in a group. Les was a natural at getting the kids' attention and encouraging them no matter how much they struggled to pick up the skills. They always seemed to pay close attention.

The clinics he took were straightforward too. At each school Favell would do the talking and I'd demonstrate the strokes, which was strange given I was a stone-waller whose first instinct was to survive each ball. Still he was 54 by then.

We normally visited two schools in the morning and then we'd adjourn to a pub for lunch for a mixed grill and a butcher of beer. It was always a butcher and no more for Les. I asked him whether when he was on tour he'd just had one beer.

'Always one butcher, that's all I needed.'

I can imagine him sticking to this mantra while the younger players in the team were out on the town. I had the feeling Les had been level-headed since he was young.

I kept bringing the topic back to his days of wearing the baggy green cap. (If ever there was someone who looked right in the baggy green it was Les.) And back to the subcontinent. I asked him about that hundred at Madras in 1960.

'I'm the only bloke whose only Test hundred wasn't a hundred at all. The scorers got it wrong and gave me a 101 when I was till on 99. I was out next ball and so the hundred stood.'

Like many of the topics we spoke about I can't remember how he managed to have the extra runs acknowledged to him. The scoreboard had got it wrong, inadvertently accelerating his score as he neared three figures. With all the fanfare as his hundred appeared on the scoreboard, perhaps the official scorers were pressured to adjusting their books.

But there it is in the history books, Les Favell 101

against India, stumped Kunderan bowled Nadkarni. It was an uncharacteristic innings for Favell, who took all day to score his ton. He was dismissed without adding to his total the next day.

Favell was a modest man. Not many people would admit that their only Test hundred wasn't a hundred at all. He went on to talk about his troubles in handling some of the Indian bowlers, one in particular. 'That was the tour where I was bowled out twice in one game by a bloke who would have had trouble getting your grandmother out. The guy was so slow through the air, I could have changed my mind three times and still played a shot. Maybe that was the problem: I had too long to make a decision.'

I knew all about embarrassment, but not on the scale that Les was talking about. At one school we went to, Les saved me from humiliation. I was supposed to be demonstrating the cover drive and completely missed one of his underarm lobs. The ball clanged into the metallic stumps behind me.

'We did that on purpose to teach you that you have to watch the ball.' Les looked at me smiling, but what he thought may have been another matter.

When I revisited his book I discovered he'd hit the runs that helped Australia win the Ashes in 1958-59 on his adopted home ground of Adelaide Oval. (He was originally from Amcliffe in New South Wales.) He'd also captained Sobers in the Sheffield Shield-winning season of 1963-64 where the Barbadian had scored 973 runs and taken 47 wickets. Like his team mate Jarman, who'd coached me, he was fulsome in his praise of the West Indian great. 'Sobers was the best all-rounder in the history of the game by a long way. He was world class at whatever he tried his hand. And his catching was out of this world. He took one catch at leg slip where he caught a ball and threw it in the air before we knew what had happened.'

I wondered if some of Favell's guidance and influence might rub off on me. Luckily it didn't take long. The Saturday after we'd finished coaching I made my highest score, 176 not out on Adelaide Oval number two for Kensington B grade. The next week, when I received a call-up to the A grade and saw him at the South Australian Cricket Association's Indoor Cricket Centre nets, he walked passed me with a big smile on his face. 'I told you this coaching would help.'

It was the last time we spoke.

The experience of coaching with Les was an education in being a good ambassador, and how to teach a love for cricket as well as some of its finer points. The summer rolled on and the school holidays ended and my contact with Les stopped. I didn't give the experience much more thought.

It was three years later when I was teaching I read that Les was dying of cancer. Closer to the end, the South Australian Cricket Association even held a testimonial match at Adelaide Oval. Some images from that game remain. There is an evocative picture of Les walking out with Sir Donald Bradman to toss the coin before the match. Les had lost his robustness of frame, but the jet-black hair and his wry smile remained. When they reached the grandstand steps, Bradman supported Les like a son would do an ageing father. There was gentleness about Bradman's touch that belied his tough exterior and showed a great deal of the respect the two had for each other.

I heard later that Les in a moment of reflection said he was saddened because he realised that this was the last cricket match he'd ever see. Perhaps for some brief moments, the still agile footwork of Neil Harvey (skipping down the wickets to play the spinners as easily as he had decades before) reminded Les of his own time in the sun and what pleasures the game had brought him. I heard that Les had been too ill to stay for the whole match.

Final walk to the pavilion, Les Favell with Sir Donald Bradman, 1987, Adelaide Oval.

By June he had passed away. I heard it on the radio on the way to school and felt saddened that such a good man had died young. Hearing the news reminded me of my brief time with Les only three summers before. It all feels like a lifetime ago and in some ways it was but the memory remains.

England's Test player Ben Hollioake was one of those cricketers who appeared to have it all. He was an elite sportsman with good looks, a charming manner and a beautiful girlfriend. Many a young cricketer would have gladly swapped places with him.

When he died at the age of 24 it was one of the biggest shocks delivered to the cricketing world. I heard the news when I was driving back from coaching an under-15 cricket team at my old school. I was no longer a teacher, having resigned after more than a decade in the classroom. Now a penniless journalism student, I had to cobble enough money together by part-time coaching and relief teaching. Financially it wasn't easy but was helped out by meals at my parents' houses. (Mum more than Dad; her cooking was still streets ahead though Dad's chicken rolls were close to perfection.)

The team I was coaching had been playing near West Beach in Adelaide. It hadn't helped that one of the side failed to show up. Even so, those who had seemed to enjoy the game. On the drive back I paused a moment and considered a quick swim at the beach. It was February and the temperature was in the mid-30s. I realised I was late for my weekly visit to Dad's house for lunch, then I heard the ABC news.

'Former England cricketer Ben Hollioake was killed earlier today in a car crash in Perth.' I pulled the car over and listened. 'Hollioake was killed when he crashed his Porsche on the way home from a family celebration.'

My mind raced back to a decade before, at Millfield College in England, one May day in 1992. 'Sir, who won the Carlton-Collingwood game?' It seemed an unlikely question from an English schoolboy who spoke with a plummy accent.

Ben Hollioake was in the Millfield under-15 cricket side I was coaching. The footy question came from the fact that he was born in Melbourne and he later went to Wesley College in Perth, but he'd moved to England with his family for some of his school years, which included his time at Millfield.

The brief coaching stint in England was 'Cardus inspired'. A few years before I had read about Neville Cardus's time as a public school cricket professional at Shrewsbury.

There he shared accommodation and stories with former Yorkshire and England all-rounder Ted Wainwright. Enchanted by Cardus's romanticised description of his life-long love of cricket, I was led to Millfield 80 years later.

The England I experienced was far removed from what Cardus described. Rather than golden sunny afternoons I often found myself standing in the middle of a freezing windswept oval, helping prepare a school pitch in the drizzling rain. The head groundsman was called 'Bushy' because of the lack of hair on his head. He was about my age but looked much older and spoke in a broad Somerset accent mostly about lager and sex in an attempt to make an Australian feel at home. Bushy's job was to show me how to prepare a pitch, which he failed dismally at. It was not for want of trying on his behalf. He eventually gave up when he saw my attempt to reverse the motorised roller. 'What the fuck are you doing?' he yelled out with a laugh before clamouring aboard the roller and banishing me to the athletics track.

Admittedly it was a beautiful background with the Mendip Hills and Glastonbury Tor in the distance. Millfield had expansive rolling fields spread throughout the town of Street at the end of the Polden Hills two miles south-west of Glastonbury. Entering the school was like walking into another world. The stately buildings of the administration area and headmaster's house reflected its nature. Millfield had the type of facilities you would normally associate with a sports academy, which in some ways it was.

But it did have its drawbacks. As one of the school's cricket 'pros' I had to respond to the request of bowling at pretentious 17-year-olds who treated you as if you were about three classes below, which I probably was. This was no school for the ordinary. African and Middle Eastern princes roamed the corridors.

By the summer of 1992 Hollioake had already played for

an England under-age team. He was tall with black curly hair, handsome, athletic and intelligent. I discovered how competitive he was when I batted one night in the nets and he peppered me with bouncers. He was only 14, but even then almost six foot tall and presented quite a prospect for the opposition batsmen.

Ben had told his team mates about how great a game Aussie Rules was. From time to time I brought the footy to practice sessions. They soon picked up the nuance of how to kick a drop and screw punt. Hollioake was a natural at all sports and managed to send a few towering kicks to his team mates at the other end of kick-to-kick. They seemed disappointed when the footy was put away.

I left the school in July that year and it wasn't until five years later that I saw him again. It was May 1997. I was about to leave for a trip to the United States and England when I watched Hollioake, just 19 years old, on television making a spectacular debut for England in a one-day match at Lord's. It was an inspired choice and a vote for English youth; he was selected after just five first class and 21 one-day games.

If ever there was a 'Cardusian' moment for flowery descriptions, this was it. On a beautiful spring day and batting at number three, Hollioake scored 63 off 48 balls, winning the man of the match award as the England side took a 3-0 sweep of the one-dayers. Hitting Glenn McGrath for 14 in one over and sweeping Shane Warne for six provided the press with enough to write him up as the next big thing. The English papers glowed with photos of that sweep.

Later that year he debuted for England with his brother Adam, becoming the fifth set of brothers to play a Test for their country. Ben showed promise with a first innings score of 28. His Test debut made him the youngest English player since Brian Close's selection in 1949. I had tickets to the final day of the Oval Test match, but it was over in four days,

Australia completing a 3-1 series win with a 264 run margin.

Later that summer I watched as Ben struck a quick half century for Surrey at the Oval. A few years later he toured Australia but had few opportunities and was largely injury plagued.

The future looked bright and his career was gaining momentum again, and then came that fateful night out on a family outing farewelling his brother back to the UK.

An excess of speed and the resultant high speed crash that snuffed out the life of a young cricketer and seriously injured his glamorous girlfriend shattered the Perth cricketing community where Ben had partly grown up. In the debris of the aftermath two broken-hearted families were still asking why. It all confirmed that no matter how glamorous and successful, you weren't immune to life's dangers.

Chapter 19

Memorabilia

Australia is playing Pakistan in a Test match; the sound of the television commentary is part of the background noise. It's the mid-1990s and I'm sitting in the lounge room of my small two-bedroom flat reading the weekend papers. Then comes the sell from Tony Greig, the South African and former England captain. He is spruiking the latest limited edition print.

Phrases such as 'wonderful collector's item', 'not to be missed' and 'get in quick before they all sell out' are used, again and again. The items are sold as part of a limited edition but when there are 999 other copies I wonder how they define limited. The prints normally mark a milestone of a player's career and are touted as a 'once in a lifetime opportunity' to purchase your own connection with the game or a player. It's amazing how many landmark moments there are.

Greig is known as much for his trademark sell as he is for anything he achieved on the cricket field. But apparently not as well-known as Billy Birmingham's parody of him for the Twelfth Man CDs where his repartee with colleague and former Australian captain Bill Lawry features. The fact both men captained their countries and played critical roles in the lead up and development of cricket's greatest revolution, World Series Cricket, seems to have been lost.

I admit to answering Greig's clarion call for the limited edition print on two occasions, namely a picture of Adelaide Oval when Greg Blewett made a debut Test century, and in the same year a shot of Shane Warne bowling at Sabina Park at Jamaica. And that is where my fascination with limited edition prints ended. Prints are really 'manufactured' memorabilia. Nowadays there is so much of it around it can be hard to establish what has value and what doesn't.

Some of the most authentic sporting memorabilia I have seen was when I visited the home of a relative of the former Australian player Edgar Mayne. It was Mum who discovered the house doing a district nursing round. When she took me back there it was like entering Aladdin's cave. The collection of cricketing treasures was sitting on an old large wooden table in the main lounge. The curtains were almost closed, obscuring the sun, while a large lamp near a rocking chair provided enough light to read by.

As Mum and the lady who owned the collection sat and drank tea, I looked at these huge scrapbooks. They were full of newspaper clippings, mainly from the early 1900s. Cricket dominated the headlines of the crowded papers on both the front and back pages even more than today. On the eve of Test matches there were huge posters of teams.

In the corner stood the bat Mayne had used to score a double century (209) in a record first wicket stand of 456 with Bill Ponsford (248) against Queensland at the MCG in 1923. He was 41 years old. Mayne's Australian cricket cap and blazer from tours to England in 1912 and South Africa in 1921-22 were also on display. It was a young cricket lover's delight.

The hours flew by. I don't know what Mum and the lady spoke about, but I didn't really care as long as it continued. At the time I thought Mayne must have been an important Australian player. I later discovered he played only four Tests with modest results. He did play first class cricket for almost a decade managing 141 matches at a time when domestic cricket meant more and international cricket was much less frequent.

I never found out where the collection finished up, and was left wondering how many more of these parts of history remained.

Another valuable piece of memorabilia is the good old fashioned autograph.

Many give the habit of collecting autographs away when they reach adulthood yet still carefully protect their childhood set. For others the habit remains. For Les Hill, who spent most of his eighty-odd years living in Mount Gambier, collecting autographs was all about the thrill of the chase and the trade. He was also the biographer of former Australian bowler Bill Whitty and, when I met him, a recently widowed octogenarian living in a nursing home.

I'd visited Les expecting to find out more details about Whitty but discovered one of the largest autograph collections in the country.

When I arrived at his small unit he soon told me about his collection which at one stage included the autograph of every Australian and English Test player from 1877 until the 1970s. That is all except one. The only autograph he'd failed to collect was England's Lord Archie MacLaren, who refused to respond to the letters Les sent. 'It was always marked return to sender.'

The story of the Les's quest was one of research, perseverance and a lot of letter writing. Every time he found the appropriate mailing addresses he would write to players asking for three copies of their autograph. The idea was to have one to keep and a few to trade. To his surprise they wrote back. Les spoke about how much fun it was to collect the mail each day when there could be a letter and a new autograph.

Often there was also a friendly note of correspondence more often than not from the lesser-known players, expressing surprise that their autograph was being sought. Some of the correspondence continued for years.

Once he had built his collection to a reasonable size, he started trading with other collectors. This was well before the days of the internet and sites like eBay. His motive had nothing to do with making money. That said, his collection must have been worth a staggering amount. By the time I'd met Les he had slowed down and even sold some of his autographs. He was going to pass the remainder on to his son.

I stayed for the whole afternoon enjoying Les's company, breaking every once in a while for tea and biscuits. When I was about to leave, he showed me his file of articles 'yet to be published'. He had been providing a regular weekly feature to the local paper on the history of the region with, as he said, 'plenty in store for when I'm gone'. As far as I know it's still going. As for Whitty, we barely spoke about him at all.

A few months after my visit Les sent me a photocopied version of his book about Bill Whitty. He included a piece of paper with three of his own autographs.

Chapter 20

An Encounter with the Golden Age

It's odd how sometimes life moves in circles. One of Edgar Mayne's team mates on Australia's controversial triangular tour of England in 1912 was Bill Whitty. Both were also team mates for South Australia and corresponded at least until 1957 when a sepia toned pictorial postcard of Whitty wearing a South Australian blazer revealed a short note from Mayne:

'Many thanks for the cuttings. Always send along anything of interest in the sporting world. Will have to try to get to Adelaide for Xmas. Am fed up with the cold weather and longing for some sunshine.'

They had more in common than an enduring correspondence. Like Mayne, Whitty experienced limited opportunities at Test level and accumulated an impressive collection of memorabilia.

Whitty was one of those golden age cricketers who played in the shadow of names like Victor Trumper, Monty Noble and Warwick Armstrong. He played only 14 Tests but was part of the first-class scene for more than two decades and took 65 Test wickets at 21. He played first class cricket from 1906 to 1926, during a tumultuous time of change in the power balance between players and administrators.

Whitty was 21 when he debuted for New South Wales from Sydney's hard wicket competition. It was an unusual move triggered by Trumper, who had heard about Whitty's uncanny sense of accuracy and ability to swing the ball late. Trumper informed NSW selector and teacher George Barbour and Whitty was asked to bowl to the state squad. Where his unwashed shoes let him down, his bowling didn't. Picked for NSW against Queensland in November of 1907, he must have had one of the most rapid rises in cricket history. In his first match on turf he took just three expensive mainly tail-end wickets.

Despite this, word of Whitty's abilities spread to South Australian captain Clem Hill, whose team hadn't won the Shield for more than a decade. South Australian cricket officials were looking for a replacement for interstate recruit, Arthur McBeath and for a complement for fellow NSW left arm paceman Jack O'Connor. They soon persuaded Whitty to cross the border.

The rise and rise of Whitty's career continued when he was selected in Australia's 1909 team to England. Surprisingly he nudged out tour hopefuls all-rounder Gerry Hazlitt and left-armer Jack Saunders. How much of a role his state captain and Australian selector Clem Hill played in his rapid progression to international status has never been revealed but there is little doubt of the influence of cricketing politics.

The relatively new Board of Control had been formed in 1905 and as a body was desperate to reduce the influence of senior players who previously controlled overseas tours. In a political ploy they appointed Peter McAlister as vice-captain and tour treasurer. McAlister's Test record was mediocre and the selection caused derision from senior players. It also meant there was now no room for South Australia's Edgar Mayne, who on performance should have been included, having averaged 49 that domestic season and scored a century in a Test trial designed to finalise the side. Queenslander Roger Hartigan was justifiably included on the basis of his Test record and an acknowledgement from the Board of the support of the Queensland Cricket Association.

For team balance the final place needed to go to a bowler. That summer Whitty had taken only 11 wickets at 49 in seven first class matches for South Australia. But Hazlitt was out of favour with Australian captain Monty Noble, after his careless fielding had cost Australia an Ashes Test the season before. The average age of those already selected (30 years) also helped Whitty's cause. Despite his inexperience he could bowl long spells and act as a workhorse on a lengthy tour, enabling senior bowlers to rest in county games.

In 1996 I visited Whitty's surviving children Bill and Ann in Tantanoola in the south-east of South Australia where their father's collection of memorabilia was stored. As I drove up the gravel path to the Whitty's front door, I imagined Bill, the old sporting hero, setting up house with his new wife. It was a dream he had harboured for many years. The house was typical of the sturdy brick homes built before the War, with room at the front of the property so that incoming guests were seen well before they arrived at the front door.

Bill junior welcomed me. After a few questions he became expansive and soon dragged out his father's old Australian cricket blazer and cap, ignominiously buried in the bowels of an old white sack. They looked their age. The blazer had retained its darkish green colour while the cap bore little resemblance to today's baggy green. They were surprisingly small given Whitty's physical stature. Maybe they had shrunk with time and wear or were weather-beaten because of Bill's tendency to wear them to ward off the biting winter chills when he was milking cows.

There was also the ball Whitty used to take his best ever Test figures of 6-17 against South African at the MCG in 1910-11. Such a small item was still so significant. A picture of Whitty hangs in a sunlit room next to the kitchen. Whitty looked like he was about to release the ball in an explosive manner. It was as if a piece of invisible elastic was tied to his hand, stopping him from releasing the ball.

As far as I know no footage of Whitty's bowling action is

'All poetry', Bill Whitty, 1909.

available. Fluent is the word most used by writers of his time to describe it. Cricket writer Johnny Moyes wrote of Whitty's action: 'all poetry… a delightful bowler to watch'. The other, more distant photo revealed as much about the standards of photography as it did about the play.

The centrepiece of the collection was a tablecloth featuring the signatures of many of key players of the time. Some were fading but they were still distinguishable. The signatures of WG Grace, Rhodes and Jackson decorated the greying cloth, while players from the triangular tournament such as Hobbs, Spooner, Woolley, Warner, Macartney, Bardsley, Faulkner, Taylor, Schwarz and Nourse also featured. Bill junior described how on the night of the dinner his father sat at Grace's table, raising a humorous speculation about the conversation between the gruff Australian and the giant of English cricket with his long beard and high-pitched voice.

Then there was the scrapbook from the 1909 tour. The black and white pictures encased in fading green covers told the story of the 1909 tour of Monty Noble's Australians to England. The man behind the album, Frank Laver, was driven by a loyalty to his players and his own passion of photography that stretched until 1919 when he took his last shots, in the Northern Territory, where he owned a property at Brunette Downs. The hardback scrapbook was beautifully presented with a dedication, and included pictures from the leisurely ship journey to England. Images from a match at Lord's show spectators in bowler hats and carriages towed by horses bringing some of the crowd to the game.

What an experience that all must have been for the 23-year-old Whitty, who had only played eight first class matches. The tour itself was a rambling affair on the ocean liner 'Orsova' with stops at Colombo, Port Said, Pompeii, Naples, Marseilles and Paris. Whitty was the baby of the team. The greatest Australian batsman of the era, Victor Trumper, took him under his wing as they toured Paris together. I wonder what they spoke about and what parts of the city they visited. It was a much more leisurely age; there were no one-day internationals to fit into a crammed and abbreviated calendar. The players visited Windsor Castle, mixed with the English aristocracy, and took in a seven-day motor tour of the north of Scotland at the end of the trip.

It was a different era. When Whitty arrived back in Adelaide there were no press conferences but rather a telegram from his employer informing him that he had to report for work that day in his job as a travelling salesman.

Whitty returned from England with just one Test match under his belt but a vast amount of first class experience. His tour figures included 77 first class scalps at an average of 20. Whitty also learned the meaning of English summer, where he'd seen more rain than any Australian winter.

From speaking with those who knew him I got the impression Whitty didn't suffer fools gladly and reflection was something you saw in the mirror. I heard his voice on an old record. He sounded weary and spoke in a deliberate manner. He described how the Yorkshire and England fast bowler George Hirst showed him how to make the ball swing. Whitty distinguished between swerve and swing: 'swerve consisted of the movement soon after the ball left the bowlers' hand while swing was late movement.' The latter sounded a lot like reverse swing, being described more than 80 years before the Pakistan team used it so effectively in a controversial Test series against England in the early 1990s.

Victor Trumper had great respect for Whitty and gave him one of his bats, which is also part of the collection. Trumper had good reason to rate Whitty; after all, he had been dismissed seven times in five matches by the left-armer.

Another large and framed photo hangs on the Whitty's spare room wall above a desk full of papers. It stands out like an Australian flag hoisted on top of a house. The picture is of the MCG in the summer of 1910-11, the scene of Whitty's greatest triumph. Like the photos in Laver's album, the shot is distant compared to today's close up colour images. But you can make out that a wicket has fallen and the left-arm bowler is about to celebrate.

How Whitty transformed from a wicketless one-Test player to a penetrative opening bowler in such a short time is worth some speculation.

Australia's summer of 1910-11 promised a lot for cricket fans. It was the first time an international side other than England toured to play Test matches. The South Africans arrived with reputations enhanced, having defeated England on their home soil with its development of a quartet of googly bowlers (Reggie Schwartz, Bert Vogler, Sid Pegler and Aubrey Faulkner). As it turned out it wasn't the googly that provided batsmen with the most trouble that summer. It was the Australian pace duo of Bill Whitty and 'Tibby' Cotter who dominated the series while the South African spinners had trouble adjusting away from matting to the harder turf wickets in Australia.

Comparing Whitty with Cotter, the only Australian cricketer to die in the First World War, makes for interesting reading. Both were Sydney boys who developed close relationships with Trumper and each had a certain respect for authority. Cotter had clashed with the newly formed Board when they took control for the 1905 tour. According to his son, Whitty had physically clashed with Cotter (then a senior player) on the 1909 tour over the way payment was to be distributed.

Yet they were also very different. Whitty was Catholic, Cotter a Protestant. Whitty was kept out of the AIF because of a knee injury. Cotter joined up as a stretcher bearer having been rejected by the Light Horse because of his eyesight. Whitty survived his pre-war contemporaries while Cotter perished at Beersheba, aged 33. Cotter's loyalty to his mates was obvious during the war, when he could have opted for a position away from danger (at one stage he was promoted to

Lance Corporal). Whitty's loyalty, at least to his team mates, could at times be called into question, as we shall see later.

In the summer of 1910-11 they worked well together. Whitty led the Australian bowling averages, taking 37 Test wickets at an average of 17. Cotter took 22 wickets at 28. They also shared the stage with Trumper, who scored 664 runs at 94.Whitty's was a spectacular performance from a bowler with limited international experience against a strong South African batting side that amassed three scores over 400 in the series.

Expected to be one of the mainstays of the Australian attack the next season, mysteriously his form fell away. Taking just three wickets at 61 in the first two Tests, Whitty was dropped from the side as the Australian selectors tried to stop a series defeat. (They failed and the home side lost 4-1.) An attack of appendicitis in the lead up to the season, requiring two operations, may have affected Whitty's fitness and his ability to bowl for long spells. He may have become complacent after his success against South Africa, or simply been overwhelmed at the strength and depth of the batting line-up of the English team, which included names such as Wilfred Rhodes, Jack Hobbs, Phil Mead and Frank Woolley.

That season there was also an escalating tension between administrators and players that eventually led to a major dispute that disrupted Australia's selection for the 1912 tour of England. The quarrel over management and the new Australian cricket authority had been building since the formation of the Board seven years earlier in a move to wrestle back control of overseas tours from the players (who had until then organised the tours and controlled the finances). A fight between the Australian captain Clem Hill and fellow selector Peter McAlister in the NSWCA offices over who would select the manager for the upcoming tour made headlines. It was simply a sign of what was to come. By the end of the summer the Big Six, (Trumper, Hill, Armstrong, Ransford, Carter, and Cotter) had decided to boycott the tour. Yet Whity surprisingly appeared passive in publicly standing up for the players' rights.

Les Hill, in his biography of Whitty, left it an unexplored subject and all the players associated with the tour are now long dead. I decided to spend some time in the reading room of the Public Library of South Australian looking at minutes from SACA meetings of the time. I found it strange reading the original documents. The committee meeting books were dusty, as though they hadn't been opened for many years (which I'm almost certain they hadn't). Opening the books with the notes in small cursive writing provided a link to the past.

I soon discovered that Whitty's state committee 'endorsed the actions of its delegates on the Board of Control, protesting against the proposal to appoint a Board representative instead of a manager' (for the 1912 tour of England). It further added, 'it is considered that the resolution is illegal (by the constitution) and almost amounts to a gross breach of faith.' It was a show of support for the players in their battle and an acknowledgment that the Board had been dishonest in its dealings with the players.

Whitty therefore had the support of his Association and admitted to agreeing with sentiments of the Big Six yet he didn't sign the letter of the boycotting players. Perhaps Whitty didn't consider himself senior enough to be included, although Macartney and Bardsley, both more senior players, also did not sign. Perhaps in Whitty's case it was self protection. That season he was averaging a modest 40 with the ball after taking only twenty wickets. His standing in Australian cricket had fallen from the lofty heights of the previous summer, yet he made the weakened 1912 Australian team to tour

England. It's unlikely we will ever know exactly why he didn't sign the players' letter of boycott, but we know he wasn't alone. It was the first of a number of Australian teams to be labelled as 'worst ever' to tour England. In many ways they lived up to it.

The Test series had a revamped format. The triangular tournament was the brainchild of Sir Abe Bailey, a wealthy cricket patron who had made his fortune through mining and pastoral activities. He owned the *Rand Daily Mail* and was later a politician. Most significantly, Bailey helped form the Imperial Cricket Conference, a forerunner to the International Cricket Council.

The tour was disrupted by poor weather (one of the wettest since records began in 1776) and modest performances by the Australians. They won only nine of their 36 first class matches. Despite this, Whitty returned to Australia with his reputation enhanced, although he never played for Australia again. He finished the tour with 25 Test wickets at 19 including a seven-wicket haul against England in the Oval Test.

The First World War ended hopes for an Australian tour to South Africa, for which Whitty had been chosen, prematurely ending his international career. He continued to play first class cricket after the War, although four years away from domestic cricket and a knee injury (which kept him out of the AIF) took its toll. Whitty continued working as a travelling salesman for the cigarette company G and R Wills until a falling out with the owner saw him move to Mount Gambier permanently. There he lived in the Jens Hotel and worked as a barman.

Whitty commuted to Adelaide to play first class cricket but was never the same bowler, eventually finishing in 1925-26 with 475 wickets. When he retired Whitty worked for six months at his sister's dairy farm based at Warwick Hill

Racetrack. During the summer he returned to Mount Gambier to play cricket. It was during this time Whitty met his future wife who nursed him during his recovery from cancer of the jaw. The couple married and moved into the dairy farm at Tantanoola Whitty had purchased just before the war. They soon produced two children: Bill jnr and Ann.

Whitty continued playing cricket well into his fifties, terrorising local batsmen with his guile and pace off the hard wickets. He was the last surviving member of Australian cricketers from the 'golden age' when he passed away in 1974, aged 87. The Whitty Shield is contested each year in the south-east of South Australia, acknowledging his contribution to cricket in the region.

Chapter 21

Cricket in Australia beyond the Traditional Boundary

I'm looking for my car. It's dark. No light anywhere. I know I parked it somewhere near here. I'm at the Alice Springs Telegraph Station several kilometres north of the town. It's now a tourist attraction, but was once used to relay messages from Adelaide to Darwin. It was also a World War II base and an Aboriginal reserve. Positioned just off the North Stuart Highway, it's now a great place to have a barbecue. I'm here to celebrate the national indigenous cricket carnival, the Imparja Cup, an event I've been reporting on for the *Centralian Advocate.* There's an official dinner but I'm also here to appear at a makeshift tribunal for a player reported for bringing the game into disrepute. That's often how things work in Alice Springs, even for a national carnival backed by Cricket Australia. For events to get up and running it's a matter of all hands on deck.

It's a hot summer night in mid-February, the temperature hovering in the mid-thirties. The usual striking illumination of the moon is obscured by thick clouds. The night is black, pitch black. The evening's formalities have ended. I am one of the last to leave and walk into the car park. The lights that lit the area for the barbecue have been turned off. I suddenly realise I've lost my way and start to feel agitated. I could be here all night. With an enormous sense of relief I hear people speaking in the distance and then see some headlights. It's one of the officials from Cricket Australia. He offers to drive me around the car park to find my car.

The story is about getting lost and seeing no way out. It's a useful analogy for describing the state of cricket in Aboriginal Australia. At the moment it's just making its way out of the darkness and at last finding a voice. Writer Bernard Whimpress's book *Passport to Nowhere* explores why so few Aboriginal players have made it to first class ranks. Halfway through his research he realised he was asking the wrong question. He should have been asking why the six or so who played first class cricket managed to make it that far.

When I first arrived in Alice Springs I had never heard of this cricket carnival for Aboriginal men and women. Word is gradually seeping out and I've written twice about it for the now defunct *Wisden Cricketers' Almanack Australia*. The ABC cricket commentator and Fairfax columnist Peter Roebuck even made his way to the Centre for a fly-in fly-out look in 2007. The newly formed National Indigenous Television station (NITV) now broadcasts matches.

Promoting cricket in the Northern Territory is a big challenge. This is a place where traditional Aboriginal games have, it is argued, resembled Australian Rules football. The most obvious example is the sport of marngrook. Some historians view it as the game that Aussie Rules is based on. Others see this theory as romanticised and politically correct for troubled interventionist times in Aboriginal communities in Australia, particularly the Northern Territory.

Either way, football dominates when it comes to its popularity in indigenous communities. Footballs and, to a lesser extent, basketballs flourish in these remote areas. The sight of a cricket bat is rare, although that's changing in places like Darwin, Alice Springs and Katherine, where local competitions thrive.

Given the amount of sports played in Aboriginal communities it's something of a mystery why cricket isn't more popular. If the battle for the 'hearts and minds' is to be won, Twenty20 cricket may be the key.

A comparison of participation of football to cricket in these communities is striking. Especially when you look at the relatively high percentage (12 percent) of indigenous players registered at AFL clubs compared to those playing grade or first class cricket (less than one percent).

The encouragement and embracing of Aboriginal footballers fostered in many ways by former Essendon coach Kevin Sheedy has not been adopted by other major sports. Given the challenges facing some communities and the support often required to transition a player from Alice Springs or Darwin to bigger cities like Melbourne and Sydney, it's little wonder the Aboriginal presence is smaller in other premier sports. As more indigenous cricketers make it to first grade ranks, numbers at the grass roots level will continue to grow, but it is still yet to be seen if cricket is a game that will endure.

If you look down the list of first class players in Australia there is a predominance of Anglicised names, apart from the occasional import. The rare cases where Aboriginal players have played first class cricket they have names such as Alec Henry and Eddie Gilbert. The list typifies in many ways the approach of cricket authorities in Australia to selling the game. But it also mirrors a society which denied indigenous peoples the right to vote until 1962, among other mistreatments.

I remember reading about Eddie Gilbert in an article by David Frith. In the mid-1970s Frith had searched for the former Queensland quick who once had the measure of Don

Bradman. It was thought that Gilbert was dead, but Frith tracked him down wandering the corridors of a psychiatric ward of the Wolston Park Hospital near Brisbane. He was a tragic figure who was then essentially incoherent and died in 1978, not long after Frith found him.

Eddie Gilbert was unusual in Australian cricket. He was a gifted athlete who lived in the Barambah (Cherbourg) Reserve north of Brisbane. He lived in a time when Aboriginal culture was incarcerated under the Queensland Aboriginal Protection Act. This meant Gilbert needed written permission to leave the Aboriginal community where he lived. It was remarkable he played as much first class cricket as he did: twenty-three matches. Controversy surrounded his bowling action: Gilbert was called for throwing 13 times by one umpire, Andy Barlow.

His chances of playing for Australia were restricted by racist policies which circumscribed his life. Gilbert was dropped from the Queensland side at the end of the 1935-36 season, having taken 5-109 and 1-33 in his final match. He was later unable to adjust to the transition between life on and off Cherbourg. His excessive drinking and womanising contributed to the growing sense of reluctance from reserve superintendent Porteus Semple to give Gilbert leave from the settlement. With 87 first class wickets at 28.97 Gilbert's career ended as a footnote rather than a highlight of Australian cricket's history.

Times have changed and there's now even an Eddie Gilbert program to try and encourage cricket in remote communities. Queensland cricket has since replaced his small white gravestone in lot number 217 in Cherbourg with a striking headstone feature marking Gilbert's life and career. There is also a statue of Gilbert at the Allan Border Field, although surprisingly not at the main ground, the Gabba.

Queensland, initially through players at Mt Isa and now

from around the state, is one of the key regions promoting cricket among Aboriginal players. That's been reflected in the state's success at the Imparja Cup where Queensland has won five national titles in six years.

The story of the competition is a fascinating one. Its pulling power is also strong with Ian Chappell and Rod Marsh having watched the carnival. Top international umpires Daryl Harper and Simon Taufel have officiated, as has former Test medium pacer turned umpire Paul Reiffel. Soon after Matthew Hayden announced his retirement he stated one of his post-retirement aims was to promote cricket in Aboriginal communities. He soon followed it up with a visit to Alice Springs to watch the Imparja Cup.

So how did a national cricket carnival involving solely indigenous players begin?

It all began with a debate between two brothers, Shane and Mervyn Franey, and their friend, Ross Jakamar Williams, about whether Alice Springs or Tennant Creek had the best Aboriginal cricketers. In 1994 a match was staged. Alice Springs won, a dispute was settled, and a concept born.

Five years later, players from the town of Borroloola, in the Northern Territory's gulf country, were invited to join in. Control of the tournament passed from the original custodians to the Northern Territory Cricket Association. In 2000-01, when Jimmy Adams's West Indians trekked to Alice Springs, the Cup got its first big kick-along. Aboriginal delegates from Western Australia and the NT met with Australian Cricket Board officials, and it was agreed that all states and territories should be invited to take part.

Tasmania went on to win that year, but it remained a largely regional affair, bolstered by the inclusion of Darwin, Katherine and the Tiwi Islands. In 2001-02, the competition was split into two divisions, comprising six states and six regional sides. The next season it blossomed into a truly national event, featuring all eight states and territories for the first time. Cricket Australia backed the 2003-04 Imparja Cup to the tune of $25,000 and the Board's chairman officially welcomed all the players. Matches were 25-overs-a-side, culminating in a 40-over final.

Shane Franey, one of the original custodians, is stunned by how quickly the concept has taken off. 'It is unreal now,' he says. 'We had a five-year plan about how the competition would develop; now it's at a stage that we thought might have been reached after 25 years. The original idea was that it might lead to the setting up of some coaching clinics for indigenous people, and we thought that one day we might get the states involved.'

Cricket Australia's involvement in the event reflects its belated awareness of the need to sell the game beyond its traditional player base. Jason Gillespie remains the only acknowledged Aboriginal player ever to have worn the baggy green. Slowly but surely, progress is being made. The Tiwi Islands, best known for their vibrant football scene, announced a three-team cricket competition featuring Milikapati, Garden Point and Nguiu. Much credit was given to the former Test captain Steve Waugh, who has travelled to the islands and Katherine.

It's early days yet the competition's success won't be measured by the number of indigenous players who go on to play for Australia but rather by the number of Aboriginal kids living in communities running around with cricket bats and balls in hand and who can happily recite the names of Australian players.

Chapter 22

A Connection with Adelaide Oval

We all feel connections with certain places. Whether it's a house we lived in or a book or record store we used to visit. These ports of call can reveal a lot about our lives. I live in Alice Springs, where people speak about a connection with the land. It is most talked about in reference to 'black fellahs' to help explain why many stay in some communities where dysfunction can define life. But even as a 'white fellah' with no dreamtime history, the attraction of the land is strong. I hear stories of people who move to Alice Springs to stay for a while and never leave. It's often about the connection with the place.

Formed millions of years ago, the MacDonnell Ranges watch over the town, providing a constant reminder of our mortality. They form part of the landscape circling Alice Springs, also including numerous watering holes and a desert that stretches seemingly forever. I have experienced the town's harshness from the oppressive summer heat and social problems. Then just when I think I've have had enough, the winter's fine cloudless days and chilly nights arrive, bringing relief. Alice Springs's demeanour becomes softer, its vibrancy returns along with a sense of optimism.

The Central Australian surrounds are as enchanting as they are enriching. I once drove the 460 kilometres to Alice Springs from Uluru, with classical music playing loudly. It felt as if I was in another world. The occasional camel and fellow traveller were the only signs of life I saw, making it an almost mystical experience. At one point I stopped the car to stretch my legs in the forty degree heat and felt like an astronaut on the surface of another planet. Such is the power of the landscape that the connection to the Centre will remain long after one leaves.

I have a similar connection with Adelaide Oval but for different reasons. When I was young it was the home of football and cricket for the city in which I lived. When I visit nowadays I experience the same feelings as I did when eight years old, watching my first Test match. I travel the 1500 kilometres from Alice Springs to make my annual pilgrimage for the midsummer Test match. It is a reminder of a past life. No matter how many times the journey is taken, and despite the changes reflected by commercialised stands and stalls set up outside the ground, the feelings remain.

Life is all about fresh starts and, like a new year, a Test match brings the opportunity of new beginnings. Each Test opens as a clean slate, and comes with the knowledge that whatever takes place during the next five days will be written into the history of the game.

As in most spiritual experiences, I have a ritualised entrance into Adelaide Oval. I walk through the parklands surrounding the city after parking near MacKinnon Parade. It's next to the Teacher's College cricket ground where memories linger of playing cricket in a struggling team. The revamped grandstand has maintained its old-fashioned style, bringing back memories of a naïve 19 year old, full of sporting hope.

The traffic builds as I reach the busy intersection of King William Road and War Memorial Drive. Aussie flags usually hang out of vehicles approaching the grassed car parks. Gum trees lining the banks of the River Torrens look on as couples in paddleboats splash their way upstream oblivious to what is happening around them.

My pace picks up when I pass over the King William Road Bridge spanning the River Torrens. The footpath has turned into a steady stream of people. I think about two pictures from my father's photo album, that are now lost. The first is of Dad and his older brother Bob, who as young boys were pictured walking to the ground for a football final. Wrapped in winter overcoats and scarves they wear huge grins. The other is of my grandparents, taken on the same day. They are dressed formally, as if going to church. In a sense they are. Dad's parents were in their mid-40s but look much older. Living through the First World War and Depression had taken its toll.

When Test cricket comes to Adelaide, the city knows it is a big occasion. A trumpet is heard as the crowd on the hill

A spiritual home to many, Adelaide Oval 1990s.

builds. Entering the gardens and then into the ground through the Victor Richardson Gates, I pass the Moreton Bay fig trees. They were originally planted to prevent those sitting on Montefiore Hill getting a free view of Adelaide Oval. They now provide a picturesque backdrop to the southern end of the oval. As part of the evolution of the ground, the Chappell Grandstands sits in front of the Victor Richardson Gates. It is the right order of things. Despite their grandfather's sporting achievements, the Chappells' legacy was greater.

Watching cricket at Adelaide Oval is different from doing so at any other ground. At times when the pitch is on the western edge of the centre-square you are so close you can hear the players encouraging each other. On a quiet day, which interstate games mainly are, if you close your eyes it can sound like you are at a parklands match.

Unlike most Test grounds around Australia, Adelaide Oval has retained its hills, although they're shrinking. Corporate boxes have no respect for grass and are steadily taking over. The hills have a personal history for many fans. Sitting on them again is like returning to the backyard of a house you used to live in. The northern end hill was where I took my first girlfriend to describe cricket's subtleties, or that was my excuse. It really was the best chance to justify why I spent so many hours playing and talking about the game. The tactic failed.

Cricket spectators are different from the die-hard footy fans. Some go to the Adelaide Oval Test just to be seen. They normally sit in the marquees at the back of the Members enclosure. The culture is so entrenched that some even claim to have not seen a ball bowled despite 'watching' Test cricket for more than twenty years. I've never quite understood why.

For young college blokes the Members enclosure was the one place, outside of dancing classes, where we might bump into girls from other schools. A friend of mine used the

Adelaide Test against India in the late 1970s as a chance to woo a girl he had been writing poetry about for most of his final year at school. I was witness to his opening line when she finally agreed to talk to him. He asked her whether she thought Australia's debut opening batsman Rick Darling was playing across the line. Her response was a blank stare. He should have stuck to poetry.

The players warm up in the nets appearing on your right as you walk through the Grimmett Gates into the Members. The pitches look perfect and alluring to anyone who has ever picked up a cricket ball or bat. The wickets are true, hard and fast. It's not until you are closer you realise the sound of elite cricketers hitting the ball is like a gun shot. When you walk up the ramp separating the Members from the outer you arrive at a picture postcard scene.

The southern hill and the famous old scoreboard with the backdrop of the spires of St Peters Cathedral sit comfortably against the lush green outfield. It's only the relatively recent inclusion of a giant electronic screen next to the scoreboard that jars. The view from the southern corner of the George Giffen stand takes in the panorama of the Mt Lofty Ranges and the city's central buildings. It is a scene portrayed in John Goodchild's 1952 painting that provided the cover for Sidney Downer's book *100 Not Out*, which detailed the ground's history. For the most part the image remains largely unchanged (although the old Members stands are now being replaced). Before the Bradman stand was built these seats were considered prime viewing space. They still are with some Members who continue to reserve their seating there with blankets and picnic baskets, several hours before the day's play.

The press men used to sit in this stand and could be heard typing in the background, often more furiously as the day progressed. At the close of play they assembled at the back of the stand to phone through their reports. During playing hours they sat close together, sharing a collection of wooden desks near the front of the stand. On hot days large fans circulated air, providing some relief. The conditions were far removed from today's air-conditioned and elevated comfort that provides the media with everything they need, including wireless internet. What would Ray Robinson or Bill O'Reilly think about the modern media with its access to multi-camera instant replays on large screens and computer analysis of every statistic of the game?

I view the Adelaide Oval differently from many because I've been lucky enough to play there. It happened twice. The first time was for a combined school side against Tonbridge, the old school of England batsman Sir Colin Cowdrey. His fourteen-year-old son and future county cricketer Graham kept the family name in tact by scoring a hundred against an older and more experienced opposition. After many years of watching cricket from the outer it was strange to have a view from the inside. From the middle I could see my Dad and the other parents sitting in the grandstand. When the bells of the Cathedral rang they sounded much louder.

To add to the occasion Sir Donald Bradman spoke to both teams before the match. I can't remember a word he said, probably because I was too excited. It was the second time I had met Bradman. The first was when I was ten years old. He was sitting in a special seating area overlooking the ground watching a Shield match when I climbed the steps of the grandstand and asked him for two autographs. He looked a little taken aback but happily signed. As he handed the autographs over he smiled and asked, 'Do you want two of mine to swap for one of Denis Yagmich's?' Yagmich was a wicket keeper from Western Australia who had moved to South Australia to play first class cricket. It was a controversial move because it shut out local keepers. Yagmich was later signed by World Series Cricket as Marsh's stand-by where he played in regional matches. I don't know how Bradman regarded Yagmich as a cricketer but the comment was intriguing, especially from a long-standing South Australian committeeman. I still have one of the autographs which I pasted into Bradman's famous book, *The Art of Cricket*.

The second time I played on Adelaide Oval was in a game of district cricket. That day we sat in the Adelaide Oval dressing room, a space containing so much history. Looking at the table next to where we placed our bags I wondered if this was where Bill Woodfull made his famous Bodyline comments to visiting England manager Sir Pelham Warner.

The team I played for was the competition's whipping-boys. Sensing his young team might become overawed appearing at a Test venue, our captain tried to keep us calm by playing music in the dressing room. Bruce Hornsby's *The Range* album sounded out as we changed into our whites. Whenever I hear *The Way It Is*, I am returned to Adelaide Oval in 1987. Our skipper told us about the many hundreds and maybe even thousands that would show up to watch us play. We batted first and when I blinked into the sunlight while walking down the grandstand steps to open the innings, it wasn't hard to notice there was no one at the ground apart from player's parents or partners. I scored only 25, yet the memory of cover driving one ball into the western side boundary made all the anxiety about the match worth the experience. Our team scored just over 200 but we managed to win, bowling the opposition out 20 runs short of the target.

As always, after stumps the shadows on the ground lengthened and the seagulls arrived for their afternoon pilgrimage, shrieking as they took off on mini-flights. Another day's play had ended.

Chapter 23

The Appeal of Skull

He's back on the radio. His laugh arrives before he does. It sounds like Muttley from 'Wacky Races'. He'd be amused at that. Kerry O'Keeffe, the former Test cricketer and now born again cricket commentator, admits his laugh, that laugh, is his signature tune. Known as 'Skull', after a comic book hero, O'Keeffe polarises listeners. Some can't stand his theatrics; many find him the perfect radio companion when the cricket is on. His media career was reborn in the last seven years on the ABC but it seems longer. Not in a tired or boring sense where you want to see the back of him, but familiar as if he's been around your whole life. Now O'Keefe's seemingly there whenever you turn on your radio to listen to the cricket. He's a bit like an eccentric friend you've known from primary school or slightly mad uncle who drops in during the holidays.

I took a while to warm to his style but now I like listening to what he says. He injects something different into the commentary box. Part of it is fun and an ability to laugh at himself. Some of the other commentators bore me. They have simply played the same old tune too often.

O'Keeffe played for Australia twenty-four times during a

seven year period, when the team experienced fluctuating fortunes. O'Keeffe Mark 1 who played in the 1970s was young with blond, curly hair. He bounded in to bowl with a swirling action of arms and legs moving in a strange unison. His action looked unnaturally complex, but perhaps it revealed a little about the way he viewed the game. O'Keefe looked confident when he played for Australia with Chappell's band of angry men, yet from what he's revealed he

Kerry O'Keefe Mark I, 1970s.

was a mass of insecurities. Like some who came and went during the period he felt he never belonged in the highest cricketing company. How would he fare nowadays as a cricketer? Perhaps very well given his work ethic, although I'm sure his bowling action would have been changed by a well-meaning coach as he climbed through the more defined and regulated tiers of the cricket structure to the top.

The O'Keeffe I remember the most is the one who played in the Centenary Test. He was the only Australian player to score a duck in the first innings, spectacularly caught at slip by Mike Brearley off Derek Underwood. It must have hurt getting out to his opposite number. He opened the batting on a pair in the second innings, filling in for the injured Rick McCosker. Elevating O'Keeffe, who normally batted down the order, was an inspired choice. He made only 14 but occupied the crease for more than an hour and showed how easy batting in the second innings was. After being bundled out for 138 in the first innings it was just the confident start Australia needed.

O'Keeffe is a man of the '70s in many ways. He's sensitive, although you wouldn't know it at first. When he talks about his life he gives the impression of not always choosing the easiest or most straightforward path to follow. Experience counts as a broadcaster.

When he wheezed out his first laugh on the ABC's sports program *The Fat* it sounded like someone demented had been let into the expert's chair. When it continued I almost turned the television off. But then insightful comments followed and I thought I was hearing something different, a view I hadn't heard before. Since those appearances his career has been on a skyward trajectory. There are O'Keeffe CDs, books and regular appearances at sportsmen's nights. He's fast becoming an industry in himself.

Despite the success, he grates on traditionalists, who

dislike his habit of talking about things like the frustrations of opening the mini milk containers on planes as on-field milestones approach. For most he gets away with it, because he reminds us that it is just a game.

O'Keeffe commentates now with a freedom he never had as a player, as if he's relishing a second chance to perform on the national stage. Not many get that once, let alone twice. Now there is less to lose, like a batsman who's already scored a hundred.

One of O'Keeffe's strengths is that he tells a good story, often in a self-deprecating way. 'Anyone can have a poor couple of decades,' he said explaining his time in the media wilderness in the 1980s and '90s. Unlike many of the Channel Nine cricket commentary club, who are past captains, O'Keeffe has a perspective we don't often hear. It's a view from someone who played within the inner sanctum of Australian cricket but was never really accepted into it. There's more I want to find out from O'Keeffe about what the team dynamics were when he played and how it affected fringe players. He's touched on how young players were sometimes treated in the Chappell era but I'm sure there is more to reveal.

Skull has a compassionate side. He showed it when he spoke at a cricket dinner in Alice Springs. He talked about his memories of David Hookes who had died just weeks before. He told the gathering his early impressions of the left hander were tainted by Hookes's comments that the Australian leg-spinner was a good bowler before adding 'for a club player'. From this unsteady start a friendship grew and O'Keeffe described his admiration for the way Hookes not only had played the game but also developed an impressive media career. O'Keeffe thought Hookes had mellowed and was a better person in middle age. It showed in his coaching and in the way he related to the younger players. Hookes didn't see it, but Victoria went on to win the domestic competition that summer and his influence had a lot to do with it.

O'Keeffe mentioned the 1977 England tour, and how both he and Hookes were introduced to English tennis player Sue Barker. O'Keeffe was a big fan of the comely blond but Barker apparently was more impressed by Hookes; a point of which his younger team mate often made the most of. Whenever O'Keeffe knew Hookes had been out with Barker, he enquired as to whether Sue had sent her love. 'Regards,' Hookes replied. 'She sends her regards.'

Then that laugh, but this time without the energy. Skull was still grieving. You could hear it in his voice when he spoke. Perhaps it's that genuineness that shines more than anything.

Chapter 24

In Search of the Baggy Green

It's a dream I've had for years. I walk past a newsagent and my picture is on the cover of a cricket magazine. I am wearing a baggy green cricket cap. It's just like an old cricket magazine I still own. On it there's a photo of Ian Chappell sweating after a long innings. He's taking his cap off and his shirt is partly undone to expose his chest. (The cover is lost now as part of a misplaced move to stick them into a scrapbook, which has since gone missing.) That dream alternates with one where former Australian off-spinner Tim May is wearing the Australian cap on the cover. These are the dreams of a teenager long ago. Oddly they resurface from the murky depths of consciousness decades later, normally during the lead-up to cricket season.

These dreams derive from an overriding passion to one day wear the baggy green cap and open the batting for Australia. Their genesis was in part an annual schoolboy's cricket carnival where I was run out three times in one week by May. He was our captain and the star off-spinner who later that year toured Pakistan with the Australian under 19 team.

It was a sign of what would follow. May played 24 Test matches for Australia and perhaps should have played more.

The closest I got to having my own baggy green was buying a closely matching replica from the internet; a leftover from a charity cricket match.

The baggy green's stocks have grown enormously in the last decade. It is now more revered than respected. You have to play for your country to receive one. Either that or buy one, often at exorbitant rates. They cost little to make but attract enormous sums of money on the market. One of Bradman's caps from the 1948 Invincibles tour sold for more than four hundred thousand dollars. The cap has taken on a talismanic significance to Australian cricketers. Only one is issued to each player and replacements given out sparingly. Hence the worn and tired-looking caps seen on the heads of experienced players.

The baggy green has come to signify more than a cricket cap. It represents a way of playing the game. Debut players are presented with their cap on the morning of their first Test. The ceremony aims to show that newcomers are a key part of the team. Steve Waugh continued the reinforcement of the baggy green tradition by ensuring all the Australian players wore it when they first took the field. The players equipped with their baggy greens became the cricketing equivalent of an invading army; unified by appearance and a force to be reckoned with.

Perhaps one of the secrets to its mystique is that it hasn't been commercially sold off. Unlike some sporting crowns such as the New York Yankees baseball cap or the skullcap English version, the baggy green remains largely unobtainable for most of us. Surprisingly, its history is just over a hundred years old.

The Australian cap hasn't always been green. It used to be blue and gold. The new colours of green and gold were adopted in 1899 after South Australian cricket administrator Mostyn Evan argued the colour represented the native gum trees. The cap has also changed in design over the years. Early versions were based on the tight fitting English caps with small peaks. By 1920 the cap was no longer made from velvet but Australian wool. It had also taken on a looser fit to reflect the fashion of the day. When Australia toured England in1938 it had reverted back to the skullcap. This bothered my friend Nick so much he wrote to former Australian captain Bill Brown asking why. Brown responded in a neat handwritten note saying as far as he knew the changes were to emulate the English cap. It was also warmer and tucked in more easily for a neat fit.

Unlike other sporting trademark items, the baggy green has remained immune to corporate logos. This perhaps more than anything explains the mythical status the cap now holds. The term has come to stand for the culture of the Australian Test cap, much like the slouch hat helped define the Australian soldier.

Although we don't like to admit it, the sight of a baggy green can automatically transform grown men into boys again and bring out a flush of feelings associated with striving to win the honour. Secretly we'd all like to have our own baggy green. My replica cap hangs off the bedpost like an old weapon whose days are over. The giveaway is that it looks, as it is, completely unused. Not quite the real thing; in fact, it's not even close.

I was involved in this type of deception before. Mum once knitted me a short-sleeved jumper with Australian colours. I was fourteen at the time and wore it to school cricket practice. In the end it wasn't worth it. I got so much grief from my classmates that the sweater was relegated to my wearing it only when I practised shots in front of the mirror.

My cricketing mate Graham was once lucky enough to

field for Australia during an Adelaide Oval Test match. For a few precious minutes he wore what we'd all been trying to wear for years. He was an A-grade district cricketer and working on the South Australian Cricket Association staff when he got the call to be 13th man. The SA side was playing interstate and injuries to two Australian fieldsmen meant my friend's relaxing afternoon hobnobbing in the dressing room changed dramatically. I was sitting in the Members stand when I heard Graham's name mentioned on radio as he ran onto the field. He survived the few overs before the fieldsman returned without embarrassing himself and at least it gave him boasting rights for the rest of his life.

When you're young the idea of earning a baggy green cap represents the ultimate goal in life. You tend to think it's easily achievable if you just apply yourself. What you don't realise at the time is how hard it is to get to that level. You discover later that the competition is so tight that it's only the best players in your school competition who might play A-grade district cricket if they apply themselves. State and Test cricketers are another breed altogether.

I know this because I was one of those kids who some people tipped would play for Australia. I didn't get close. It wasn't through lack of trying. I worked harder than most at the game and played cricket at grade level before realising I lacked the necessary confidence and probably the talent as well.

As my Dad used to say, 'It's not everyone that gets the chance to open the batting for Australia.'

He was right.

Chapter 25

The Road Ahead

Looking ahead I wonder whether the quest to wear the baggy green will continue to be as strong. Will it be simply a matter of wanting to become part of cricket's high-paying franchises that have started to form in Twenty20 competitions?

A hint of what cricket's future may hold was revealed when more than eighty thousand fans turned up to the Melbourne Cricket Ground for Australia's Twenty20 clash with India in February 2008. English sports writer Simon Barnes, in reference to the new game, wrote that 'Cricket has become the great disappearing game,' but perhaps he was referring simply to the future of Test cricket. The latest abbreviated form of cricket is fast becoming the richest game in town. Franchises in the Indian Premier League sold for multi-millions of dollars, with cricket becoming more global and less national. Twice the number of Indian fans tuned in to watch the IPL than the India-South Africa series in the same year (2008). When the money speaks, patriotism keeps quiet.

You now don't have to imagine a scenario where an Australian fringe Test player attracts up to ten times his annual salary by opting to play in a series of Twenty20 matches. It's already happening.

The trend raises the question as to what will happen to the standard of first class and Test cricket when alternative lucrative competitions gain even more prominence and start skimming cricket's cream?

Cricket's administrators have responded quickly, with sanctioned lucrative Twenty20 competitions appearing at quarantined parts of the cricketing calendar.

A dilemma will also exist for coaches. Will young players be brought up learning the skills it takes to play for two days, or twenty overs?

Just as has happened in elite football, a physical prototype will most likely emerge. The top game accessible to players of all builds will no longer be so. Cricket could become a game at elite level for players who are tall, angular, athletic with ability to hit the ball a mile, field exceptionally and be able to bowl some containing overs. It will be a world for players like Andrew Symonds and Kevin Pietersen. Maybe, as in other sports, cricketing bodies will start fast-tracking teenagers with the necessary attributes.

Where will Test cricket fit into this changing world? After all enthralling contests continue to take place. Yet attendances for Test matches outside Australia and England are relatively poor, pitifully so in some countries. Will the longer form of the game become a quaint reminder of things past, or stay as the foundation of cricket around the world? My hope and belief is that Test cricket will always be valued; it is after all the game in its purest and at times rawest form. Its memories are the ones we cherish. There is talk of a world championship featuring stronger Test-playing nations and even day-night Test cricket, although there is a general unwillingness of cricket administrators and commentators to accommodate the latter.

One of traditional cricket's saving graces is that the abbreviated variants of the game fail to satisfy younger players in the way its predecessor has. Slogging a quick fire 30 in a Twenty 20 match has appeal but doesn't compare to crafting out a well made hundred. For bowlers the short form of cricket is increasingly demoralising.

Yet it's probable that the future of cricket will not be decided by those raised on Test cricket but rather a diet of two Twenty20 matches in one afternoon, given large exposure through international broadcasting networks complete with high-charged entertainment during the change of innings. It's the cricketing purists who may have to concede the changing face of the game, either persisting with it or leaving.

Ultimately cricket is evolving, as it always has and always will.

Order your copy

		Qty
Cricket Dreaming ISBN 9781921221897	AU$24.95*	……
Postage within Australia	AU $6.00*	……

TOTAL __________

*All prices include GST

Name: ………………………………………………………………

Address: ………………………………………………………………

………………………………………………………………

Phone: ………………………………………………………………

Email: ………………………………………………………………

Payment: ❑ Money Order ❑ Cheque ❑ Amex ❑ Mastercard ❑ Visa

Cardholder's Name: ………………………………………………………

Card Number: ………………………………………………………

Expiry date: ………………………………………………………

Signature: ………………………………………………………

Allow 21 days for delivery.

Payment to: Better Bookshop (ABN 14 067 257 390)
PO Box 12544
A'Beckett St VIC 8006
Fax: 03 9671 4730
admin@brolgapublishing.com.au

Be Published

Publishing through a successful Australian publisher. Brolga provides:

- ✔ Editorial appraisal
- ✔ Cover design
- ✔ Typesetting
- ✔ Printing
- ✔ Author promotion
- ✔ National book trade distribution, including sales, marketing and distribution through Macmillan Australia

For details and inquiries, contact:
Brolga Publishing Pty Ltd
PO Box 12544
A'Beckett St VIC 8006

Phone: 03 9662 2633
Fac: 03 9671 4730
bepublished@brolgapublishing.com.au
markzocchi@brolgapublishing.com.au
ABN: 46 063 962 443